Aussie Classic
CAR FINDS

Aussie Classic
CAR FINDS

HOLDENS, FORDS, CHRYSLERS, MORE

A Gelding Street Press book
An imprint of Rockpool Publishing Pty Ltd
PO Box 252
Summer Hill
NSW 2130
Australia

geldingstreetpress.com

ISBN: 9780645207064

Published in 2022 by Rockpool Publishing

Design and typesetting by Sara Lindberg, Rockpool Publishing
Edited by Lisa Macken

Stories and images originally published in *Survivor Car Australia* magazine

 A catalogue record for this
book is available from the
National Library of Australia

Printed and bound in China
10 9 8 7 6 5 4 3 2 1

CONTENTS

INTRODUCTION

In the classic fairy tale Sleeping Beauty is cursed to sleep for 100 years, only to be awakened by a handsome prince and saved from her desperate situation. We cannot claim the sleeping beauties in this book were set free by handsome princes, but awoken from long slumbers they most certainly were. Every car enthusiast has dreamed of finding the object of their desire – of the automotive kind, that is – and *Aussie Classic Car Finds* tells the stories of many such machines.

The book uncovers automotive treasure from across the nation such as Holdens, Fords, Chryslers and other Australian-built or delivered classics that are often derelict, rare and valuable, and unlocks a unique human-interest story with each discovery. Consequently, these dirty, dusty and dilapidated cars are of great interest to petrolheads despite their poor condition. In America such vehicles are called barn finds; in Australia we find them in sheds, garages, carports and paddocks. For many, a barn find is the Holy Grail of classic car ownership.

The book is divided into four parts: Awakenings, Slumbering, Going, going, gone . . . and Rescue missions. Awakenings tells of recently discovered cars, many coming out of hibernation. Slumbering features cars safely tucked away but seemingly destined to remain as they are. Going, going, gone . . . covers machines beyond the point of no return and on the slippery slope to destruction. Finally, Rescue missions details salvage operations, delicate extractions and new lives with new owners.

Most of the finds are so-called 'Survivor' cars – machines without significant modifications since new – while some others are not, but almost all are in need of attention. What they have in common are the fingerprints of history, which tell their particular story of how each one came to be in their resting place. Join us as we reveal some amazing discoveries.

Maybe you will be inspired to unearth your own sleeping beauty. It's not an impossible dream, as the cars on the following pages are testament to the fact. They're still out there . . .

Valiant/Ranger.
BY CHRYSLER.

PART I:
awakenings

HOLY MOTHBALLS!

'Barn find' is a colloquialism that is used worldwide regardless of whether it's a shed, garage, carport or in fact an actual barn. Most barn finds start out as normal cars used daily to commute to and from work or as family hacks; then, one day, a certain event takes place that changes everything. Such an event took place with the 1972 XA Falcon GT seen here, now nicknamed 'Mothball', some three decades ago.

This Red Pepper XA GT started out as a young man's pride and joy. Pat, the son of humble Italian immigrants, has a passion for fast cars. He purchased the GT brand new from Holmesford GT Zone in Melbourne and kept it until 1984 when, with around 28,000 miles on the clock, he sold the GT to his mate Mick so he had the funds to build a new garage. Mick was then a hard-working house painter, and he fell in love with the GT the first time he saw Pat driving it. Pestering him occasionally, he was in the right place at the right time when Pat decided to sell. The GT was supposed to be Mick's retirement fund.

Mick had always had an interest in fast cars, and a reputation to match – losing his licence some 13 times! One time when he was driving to the annual Bathurst race he got pinched at 130 mph, only to be pinched again coming back. Mick's nickname

was 'Stickman', as he was always changing gears. He only knew two speeds: either going fast or going flat out.

Eventually Mick fell on hard times and asked his old school mate Neil if he wanted the car. 'I originally said "No, I'm not interested,"' Neil recalled, 'but he asked me three or four times, and because he needed the money I thought: *what the hell*.' For five grand and with three months rego, it was a pretty good deal for a performance car with around 55,000 miles on the clock. This all happened in May 1987, and Neil lost contact with Mick when he moved out of Melbourne.

Neil's purchase of this performance machine was somewhat unusual in that he is not really a petrolhead, unlike his lifelong mate Dave. The pair has long been inseparable. With three months rego left, Neil decided to drive the-then pristine XA GT occasionally. He remembers: 'Dave and I went out to the pub one Friday night, had a few too many beers and realised neither of us was fit to drive home so we left the GT in the carpark.' Doubting he'd do the same thing today, he said: 'We were pretty badly hung-over so we came back two days later, and it was still there!'

Neil parked the XA GT in his backyard when the rego ran out, and there it sat until the grass grew up around it. 'It sat out there for two years,' Neil said, until one day Neil's father shouted, 'What a waste, get that bloody car in the shed!' The boys pushed it into the shed, and that's where it's been

LEFT Mothball was parked up in a shed for three decades.
ABOVE It has travelled an average of just 1,000 miles per year over its first 50 years. Check out the film of dust on the windows!

mothballed ever since. In the 1990s, Neil had an in-ground swimming pool installed in the backyard and some landscaping done that blocked access to the shed. To get the mothballed XA GT out today, either a crane would be needed to lift it over the house or a big chainsaw to chop down the trees that have grown across the narrow pathway.

In the mid-1990s, when these types of cars became a bigger target for theft, Neil was advised to remove the ID plate and place it away for safekeeping.

Dave retired in 2008 and said to Neil, 'That car in the garage, you want to get it going?' The boys

started doing some research around the height of the muscle car boom. 'We went to a Shannons classic car auction, where we saw a GT-HO Phase III sell for more than $600,000 and thought: *what the hell!*' Neil and Dave exclaimed, wide eyed. 'We got that thing sitting in the shed doing nothing and it might be worth a few bob,' Neil recalled of how the adventure started. 'I had it in mind to put a fox tail on the aerial and drive it with Dave to the pub in Whittlesea, where I'm originally from.'

Neil and Dave knew they had something special but weren't sure which way to go, so they started googling to learn more about XA GT Falcons. This led them to the online Falcon XA GT Discussion Forum, where they began chatting with other like-minded enthusiasts who were stumped about some of the go-fast bits fitted to Mothball. They were soon advised what to look for and where to look.

To their amazement, Neil and Dave found the original production line build sheet stuffed inside

under the shocker grommet. 'It had a perforated edge, so we knew it wasn't someone's lunch wrapper,' Neil and Dave joked, adding, 'It was quite a task getting it out in one piece.' The boys were then hooked on finding out as much as they could about Mothball's history.

By sheer happenstance, Neil's son Darren went away for a weekend to the Mount Beauty snowfields in north-eastern Victoria, taking the back roads up there. He pulled up at the one-horse, one-pub town of Tatong to quench his thirst and recognised a bloke in the corner as his dad's old mate Mick, from whom he had purchased Mothball. They exchanged numbers.

Neil called Mick as soon as he found out about the chance meeting, and began asking about the engine mods on the GT. To Neil's surprise, Mick informed him that he wasn't the first owner of the XA GT and that he had bought it with around 28,000 miles on

the clock from a guy named Pat. The only clue given was that Pat lived in the Oakleigh-Moorabbin area of Melbourne. The initials on the black and white personalised number plates were PP-351, so it was assumed Pat's last name also began with a 'P'.

Neil and Dave went through the phone book and called all the last names beginning with 'P' that also began with the initial 'P' who lived in that general area, but had no luck. Fired up, Neil drove to Tatong with a Melbourne street directory in hand to see Mick, who circled the general area he thought Pat lived in.

Neil and Dave spent a couple of evenings driving through the area knocking on doors at random, again with no luck. 'We got chased by dogs and told to piss off!' Neil laughed. Neil had it in his head to drive back up to Tatong and drag Mick back to Melbourne to show him which street and which actual house Pat lived in, but then Mick remarkably remembered that the first owner worked in a panel shop with his brother in the Prahran area and he even remembered the name of the shop.

Dave called the shop thinking the owners would be long gone, but to his surprise the panel shop was still in operation. He enquired if there was a 'Pat' there who used to own a GT, and was told that he didn't work there any more but that his brother worked as a panel beater in the Bayswater area, some 30 kilometres away in the east.

'We managed to contact his brother, who gave us his last name, "Pugliese", and a contact number,' Neil and Dave said, now feeling proud of their achievement. 'Pat couldn't believe we were calling him about the GT and that it was still around. He said he'd try to find some old photos for us of when it was new.'

Pat informed the two lads that he'd originally ordered a Phase IV but was later told they were no longer available and had to settle for a standard XA GT tricked up with some Phase IV bits. Pat then said to Neil, 'I wouldn't mind seeing the old GT again if that's okay with you.'

Being reunited with an old car is much like a reunion with an old flame: you get excited and nervous at the same time, your palms start sweating and your throat gets dry as you're about to step into view. Now retired, Pat Pugliese, the original owner of the XA GT aka 'Mothball', felt much the same when he first laid eyes on his long-lost beauty. It was an OMG moment long before the abbreviation took hold.

It had been 31 years since he last saw his beloved Red Pepper XA GT, and he told the boys he wished

he had the chance to buy her back to save her from a mothballed fate.

With all the pieces of Mothball's history now in place, Neil and Dave were ready for the next step of their journey – to free her from the decades of slumber covered in dust.

For these two lifelong friends the adventure has been an enjoyable one so far, but now came the challenge of getting Mothball out of her tomb and onto the road. And it proved easier said than done, as a later chapter outlines. ▨

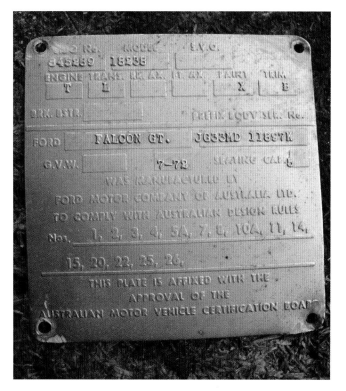

FAR LEFT This is a highly prized matching numbers car, meaning it's still fitted with its original engine. What's inscribed on the chassis matches the numbers on the ID plate (right) and engine.

TREASURE ISLAND

This is the story of a tradie who grabbed his tools one morning and headed off to work, just as he did every other day. But this was no ordinary day: this was the day he discovered a barn find.

'I had a job in Bicheno on the east coast of Tasmania,' Tassie sparky Mick Munro said. 'I was helping out my mates Andrew and Dianne Baily, who wanted a fluoro light put up in their kitchen. Andrew realised I was low on supplies and piped up, "Michael Webb across the road is an old electrician; he might have some tubes – and come to think of it, he's got an old Holden in his shed, too." Even though I'm a Ford man,' Mick said, 'Andrew knew I loved old cars regardless of their make. When I heard "Old Holden" my car radar went on high alert!'

Andrew and Mick knocked on Michael's door. Retiree Michael said: 'Call me Webby. I've got plenty of tubes in my shed; follow me.' Within minutes the three men were standing in front of a large, four-car shed. 'I remember the moment the roller door rattled up,' Mick said. 'It took a few seconds for my brain to catch up with my eyes, but then there it was: a Barbados Green HQ Monaro GTS coupe covered in crap.'

When Webby noticed Mick staring at his green GTS he said 'It's not for sale,' before Mick had a chance to offer. Mick offered $25,000 cash anyway,

taking one more admiring glance over his shoulder as the roller door slammed shut.

Mick's mate, east coast IGA supermarket owner Matt Eastwood, said: 'Mick told me all about the GTS. How it had a factory vinyl roof. Five litre L31 V8, M21 4-speed box. How it was the dealer principal's car. How the colour popped. Part of me wished he hadn't even mentioned it.' Matt took down Webby's phone number and plonked it on a spike inside his office. Five years passed.

Born and bred in Launceston, Webby was born in 1938 and secured an apprenticeship with Medhurst Electrical until he decided to freelance as a contractor on the east cost of the apple isle. With a love for the water as a champion swimmer and lifesaver, he became a fisherman for awhile and even joined the merchant navy, serving as an electrical engineer. When an opportunity came up for a position in Tonga, he opted to stay in Australia and marry his sweetheart Athalie and start a family.

A larrikin who loved a laugh, Webby bought himself an old BSA classic motorbike and later owned a Triumph that he dropped a few times. With the penny dropping he was safer on four wheels than two, an MG TC convertible came along.

With his electrical business now prospering on the east coast, Webby decided in 1974 to update Athalie's orange Mini and get her into something more flash to ferry their three children to and from school in. While on a trip to Hobart he noticed a

but Webby smiled and shook his head. Thinking Webby might consider a higher amount, Mick told him he had a mate who might offer a little more but Webby shook his head and said: 'I've got plans for her.' Mick managed to get a phone number before

bright green Monaro two-door parked at Motors, Hobart's Holden dealer. Striding in for a closer look, he was told it was the dealer principal's personal car and had been ordered nine months previously as a special order from the assembly plant in Sydney. 'Ripper,' said Webby, 'I'll take it!' It ended up ferrying the kids around for more than a decade.

The Monaro was parked up in 1986 rather than being sold as Webby knew it was going to be valuable someday; they didn't make them like this any more. The Monaro was moved from St Marys to Bicheno, where it sat for 20 years. To think the sleepy fishing village of Bicheno with its population of just 850 residents hid this gem of a classic without anyone finding out about it until it was stumbled on by Mike Munro!

Webby had good intentions of restoring the Monaro GTS but thankfully never got around to it, as it's now one of a very few Monaro GTS coupe Survivors in the country.

Matt said: 'I was still in the market [in 2015] for a GTS Monaro, but every time I got a copy of *Just Cars*

> " The Monaro was parked up in 1986 rather than being sold

and found a car I liked, I was a day late and it was sold. Then I started advertising on Gumtree and eBay and travelled to South Australia, New South Wales and Victoria but they were all crap.' Matt well remembers the lies from owners with so-called 'perfect examples'.

Mick and Matt were discussing the hopelessness of finding a Survivor GTS Monaro when Mick clicked his fingers. 'Do you still have the electrician's phone number from Bicheno?' Matt pointed at the spike on his office desk and said: 'Stuff it, I'll try ringing

him one last time!' He was called out to deal with a matter in the store and handed the phone to Mick to make the call, and remembers that: 'I walked back into my office and there's Mick with a big grin on his face, and he's giving me the two-thumbs-up signal.' Webby had told Mick he would sell. 'I was that excited I barely slept!' Matt said.

'Here she is,' Webby announced when he opened his large roller door. 'I'll kick it over.' Matt and Mick stood there like two kids in a candy shop. 'No, it's fine,' pleaded Matt. 'I'm happy to look at it as it is.' Webby persisted and disappeared back into his house. 'I was really impressed with the low-kilometre car; dumbfounded, almost,' Matt said. 'Doeskin with cloth inserts, houndstooth fabric seats, vinyl roof . . . It was a complete, unmolested car with a few day two mods.'

Webby reappeared with a small 12-volt battery. 'The wife's not going anywhere so I pinched her wheelchair battery.' Mick and Matt watched nervously as Webby tried to start the car after a 20-year sleep. He cranked it once and it strained, then suddenly the 308cid V8 suddenly rumbled into life.

'I couldn't believe it,' Matt said, although he realised that the oil may have separated and the fuel was probably contaminated. 'The car was a great example except for one thing: the paint. Tiny bubbles of surface rust had popped up under the paint in various places, but that's just part of the Survivor's story. Every time I go and look at a car I promise my wife this will be the last one – that was about five cars ago – but I've always wanted a GTS Monaro.

Sadly, a few months after Matt bought the Green Machine old Webby passed away

Always! And this was the one, so the negotiations began.

'We went backwards and forwards and eventually settled on a fair price. I had the flat-bed truck in the driveway and I wasn't going home without her. After a wash and a vacuum there wasn't much to do but enjoy her. I had the engine and drivetrain checked over and the news was all good. The 308 purrs, and the only thing that was needed was a carby kit.' To this day, the Monaro has never been off the island since arriving from the mainland when it was new.

Sadly, a few months after Matt bought the Green Machine old Webby passed away, but there's no

doubt it has gone to a good home. The GTS sits neatly next to some of Matt's other toys: Camaro, GTR XU-1 Torana and a couple more. 'All my other cars have been restored – they're like new – but this is my first Survivor car and I love it!'

According to General Motors-Holden, this car was built at the Pagewood assembly plant in Sydney on the 4 March 1974 as an HQ Monaro GTS coupe fitted with the (L31) 308cid HC V8, (M21) 4-speed floor shift and the (GV2) 10 bolt Salisbury axle with the 3.36:1 diff ratio and sold to dealer code 129, Motors Holden in Hobart.

At the time of writing it had covered just 98,667 kilometres. ■

LEFT New owner Matt hoses off decades of dust and gives the Monaro its first bath in a long time. ABOVE Just like new after a tub.

HIBERNATING HEMI

ick opened the doors of an old shed in the backyard of a house in Oberon in New South Wales's central west and could not believe what he saw. Inside was a genuine Chrysler VG Pacer that had been hibernating since 1982 under layers of brown dirt. The car had not been registered for decades. 'I was in disbelief that someone could leave a car for so long and not fix it,' Mick said. 'The stumps holding the shed up had nothing at the bottom. It was a miracle it was standing,' he continued.

The Pacer looked complete apart from a missing front grille and headlights and dried mud was caked on the car underbody. Mick had discovered it was for sale via word of mouth, and within days he had driven from Canberra to Oberon to look at the car. It had been owned by Brian McMahon since new. As it was pulled from the shed, Mick noticed the passenger door and rear guard were in primer.

Ben, Brian's son, told Mick he had sprayed the door and guard after rubbing it back for practice when starting his spray-painting apprenticeship in 1996. He had also removed the grille and front and rear lights, but the planned respray never happened because Ben turned his attention to an XW Falcon ute.

Brian had originally parked the car in the shed in 1982 when the Welch plugs started leaking and never

fixed them. A relative bought a CL Valiant so he decided to buy one as well. The Pacer sat in the shed for the next 14 years until Ben's partial undercoat, then it was put back in the shed until 2019.

The car was bought new in 1970 from Louie's in Cabramatta after Brian came home from the army. It spent the next 12 hard years racking up 95,000 miles on dusty, rocky, unsealed country roads all over New South Wales while he travelled to find work as a contract shearer. Despite its hard life, it had survived. Mick had found and bought himself

a fair dinkum barn find, and he loaded it onto a trailer.

This Pacer is very original and as rare as rocking horse droppings. It's a matching numbers car with original Pacer dash, bucket seats and trumpet horns, which were unique to this model. The spare tyre in the boot is original, along with the rare Pacer red carpet with black trim.

Mick's plan is to paint the primed areas, put back the original parts that were taken off and get it running again. The Pacer grille with its distinctive orange stripe will be refitted, along with front and rear lights. Meanwhile, original wheels will replace the period mags to make this car authentic.

Mick has had every model Valiant since 1993 and currently has nine, including four Pacers and a daily driver VG utility. He first went to the Great Race at Bathurst when he was 12 years old. 'I just had to have the Pacer as part of the golden era of Bathurst,' he said. 'This Pacer needs to live again, and needs time to get it right so it can get back on the road.'

For now this rare Survivor will stay in barn find condition until it wakes again from its long slumber. ▣

TOP LEFT The most unassuming sheds or garages can contain remarkable automotive treasure.
LEFT Valiant Pacers raced at Bathurst, a neighbouring town to Oberon where this little ripper was found.

SPORTY SPICE

Only 18 Mk8 Bolwell Nagari Sports were ever built. Packing Ford's 351 or 302 cubic inch Cleveland V8 engine, this beauty was a beast in designer clothing. The Nagari had Aussie supermodel good looks but performed as a demon due to its revolutionary lightweight body.

This magnificent Signal Red Nagari Sports (Chassis No. B8/78) started life in Mercedes Silver Metallic and rolled off Campbell Bolwell's factory floor in Melbourne on 22 December 1972. Purchased for $7,250 by Canberrian Ross Reid, it was driven sparingly for a few years then on-sold to Brian Walters, who changed the colour to Signal Red. In 1981 police officer Dennis Mitchell snapped it up and moved it to his property in Yass.

Dennis used the Nagari for the reason he bought it. After extending the roll bar to meet racing standards, he unleashed the V8 on the hill climb circuit. He competed in several hill climb and motor sport events around the Goulburn, Picton and Camden areas, but after just 18 months he parked the Nagari in the barn and never competed again.

At the same time Dennis was mothballing the car, 21-year-old Colin Watson was fresh from completing his fitter and turner apprenticeship. 'I was sitting at the lights in my LC GTR Torana when this car pulls up next to me,' Colin remembered. 'The V8 burble

was just as hypnotising as the shape. Before I could figure out what it was, it flew off. From that instant I knew I wanted one even though I didn't know what it was!'

Colin started studying all his old car magazines until he found what he was looking for. 'I went and looked at a couple but they were too expensive. One day I was driving down the street and [saw] in this opened garage a red Nagari Mk8. I immediately

ran up and knocked on the front door and said: "I want to buy your Nagari." They told me it didn't go and that the Cleveland 351cid V8 was too powerful for someone as young as me.

'I continued to nag them until they gave in. I sold my Torana and rocked up with the cash. The key had been broken off in the ignition, so I hot-wired the car and drove it home unregistered. I drove the wheels off it.'

More than thirty years passed. Colin still had the Nagari Mk 8 in the garage and was now the president of the New South Wales Bolwell Car Club. In 2017 he received a phone call, after which he phoned fellow Bolwell tragic and Nagari Sports owner Mark Cleaves. 'I've just been contacted by the owner of one of the three missing Nagari Sports!' Colin and Mark headed off to Yass to discover which of the Sports models it could be.

Dennis Mitchell's wife Joy Witton said to them: 'Dennis loved his cars. I was into horses and he was into cars. It became quite common for him to just show up with a Jag, an Alfa or in this case a Bolwell Nagari Sports. His dream car was an Aston Martin DB5. If he had found one I would have loved him to have bought it. He just loved researching and finding beautiful-looking cars.'

Colin said: 'We were very sensitive of the situation [as] we knew it was a heartbreaking thing Joy was doing. [She] took us to a barn and there it was: I was speechless. I'd seen bard finds on TV and YouTube, and I was ready for a challenge.' Mark said: 'Thirty-two years of dust is a lot of dust. You could smell mice urine throughout the car. I looked at Colin, and he was just thrilled to see it.'

The boys realised this Bolwell Nagari Sports was one of the most original examples in Australia. 'I had to have it,' Colin said. "I explained [to my wife] that her dream kitchen had to wait [because] these Nagari Sports are just so rare.'

When Colin went to pick up the car he found that Joy had pumped up the tyres and collected all things Bolwell, and she gave instructions to take anything

BELOW Fitted with a Ford Cleveland V8 engine, the Bolwell had all the grace of a ballerina wrestling a gorilla.
RIGHT It scrubbed up well!

related to the car. 'We even found the Bolwell wheels, and the original steering wheel wrapped in a timber box.' Colin rebuilt the car. 'The brake and fuel lines had corroded from mouse urine and the car was overheating, so I serviced the heads.'

Today, Colin's Bolwell Nagari Sports is a magnificent Survivor car. 'When I go for a cruise I take my 93-year-young dad for a drive. We go and see his mates and go to club meets.' ∎

THE REAL McCOY

This 1970 Ford Falcon XY GT sat exactly where it was parked up in the early 2000s: tucked away in a shed in a quiet suburban street. Even the neighbours were oblivious to its existence until it was recently dragged out and dusted off.

Its known story begins with Bernie, who had moved to Ballarat to look for work as a youngster and ended up on a farm in nearby Alfredton. He'd had the GT since the early 1970s and had used it regularly, even taking it out hunting wild pigs. Almost inevitably, he ended up clobbering a kangaroo. The car was repaired, but more care was taken as to where and how the car would be used to avoid further marsupial masochism.

Howard and his wife Karen were at a party in Alfredton sometime in 1997 when Howard's father-in-law, knowing that Howard was a car guy, mentioned Bernie's GT and asked if Howard had seen it. Howard was surprised this was the first he'd heard of it and decided to go back to have a look. A few years later Howard had a chance to see the car, which by then was up on blocks and had had bits and pieces removed. Even so, Howard made an offer but Bernie was reluctant to sell.

Howard kept an eye out for another GT over the following months when one day he saw Bernie out the front of his house. Bernie said: 'It's yours if you still want it.' Sadly Bernie had been diagnosed with

a serious illness and had decided it was time to sell up. Howard brought his new purchase home on a trailer in 2004 and parked it in the shed, and there it has stayed ever since. Big ideas of returning the car to the road got lost in the day-to-day comings and goings of life. 'I'm 60 now and it'll be still the same in 10 years,' he says of his decision to sell it on. 'We have a Burgundy XT Fairmont we would like to focus on getting back on the road instead.'

Originally sold by Bob Rollington Ford of South Yarra Victoria on 14 January 1971, the GT was delivered in Track Red although Bernie said it was already painted white inside and out when he bought it. The car came equipped with the four-speed manual and matching number T code 351 cid 4V engine, and was adorned with black

> " This Survivor GT's body shows just 87,436 miles on the odometer.

vinyl trim. It was also equipped with the desirable wind-back sunroof and integrated air-conditioning, making this a 'one of one'. Interestingly, the car was re-registered in 1975 with LYY-999 on its plates. The white paint was applied in the early seventies and a sticker on the back window suggests it was on-sold at some point through West Geelong Motors.

This Survivor GT's body is surprisingly rust free and shows just 87,436 miles on the odometer. A few areas of white paint have peeled away to reveal the car's true Track Red identity. Some of the trim and engine components have been removed and placed in the boot, but it appears to be complete. Inside dust and grime mar the surfaces, but it appears that under the grime all is surprisingly well

preserved; there were even a number of empty shell casings on the floor from the pig shooting days! An inspection of the steering wheel reveals the novel placement of five cent pieces in the steering wheel centre pad. Overall, the car was begging for a thorough detail.

Howard ended up selling the GT to Lenny, a local from Ballarat. Lenny trailered the car straight from Howard's to a local car wash on the way home, and has since replaced the bent pushrods. With a quick freshen up, this Survivor car has now been returned to the road. ▧

TOP LEFT Not even the neighbours knew this shed contained a valuable GT.
ABOVE Covered in cardboard, the GT was used as a bench of sorts.

THEY'RE STILL OUT THERE

Only 580 of the Holden HX Limited Edition coupes were built at GM-H's Pagewood assembly plant in 1976. One of these rare beasts, build number 558, sat parked at the bottom of a driveway in a country Victorian town until renowned car hunter Ross Vasse stumbled across it by chance. Admittedly, finding a forgotten muscle car these days is considered unlikely given that every man and his dog knows about them. However, they're still out there if you're prepared to put in the hard yards and go looking.

As Ross describes it, finding this HX LE coupe was a fluke. 'I was down in Leongatha following up another dead-end lead on an old car I was chasing and had some time to spare,' he explained. 'So I drove up and down every street in the neighbouring town of Korumburra. I'd driven about a dozen streets when I noticed a torn blue tarp thrown over a car at the bottom of a driveway.'

Ross stopped and reversed for a better look; he could instantly make out it was a Holden coupe. 'The colour was what really gave it away: soon as I saw that burgundy shade I thought *"Hmmm, an LE Monaro"*,' adding, 'Yeah, I know Holden never called them an LE Monaro but LE coupe doesn't have the same ring to it, does it? I knocked on the door, but no one was home. Out of respect for the

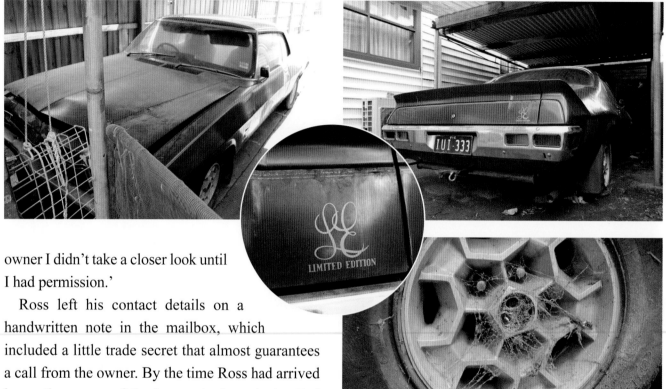

owner I didn't take a closer look until I had permission.'

Ross left his contact details on a handwritten note in the mailbox, which included a little trade secret that almost guarantees a call from the owner. By the time Ross had arrived home the owner of the house, Andrew, had called to express an interest in selling the HX LE coupe. The car belonged to Andrew's brother, who had bought it from the nearby township of Tooradin from the first owner back in the early 1980s.

The LE coupe was being used as a daily driver until one day one of the nephews came flying down the driveway in a car with questionable brakes, slamming into the front of the coupe and damaging the nose cone and front bumper. The car's owner lost interest, threw a tarp

> *The nephew came flying down the driveway, slamming into the front of the coupe.*

over the car and let it sit. After some years the tyres went hard and eventually flat and spiders and other insects claimed every nook and cranny, but if there was a recipe on what makes a barn find, then spiderwebs, flat tyres and dust would be the three key ingredients.

After a brief chat over the phone with Andrew an asking price was disclosed and a decision made for Ross to go back down the next

day for a closer look. Upon inspection and some customary haggling a fair price was agreed upon, and a tow truck arranged to collect the LE coupe.

As the car had sat idle for more than a decade the brakes were seized on, locking up all four wheels when it was winched onto the tow truck. 'It reminded me of a cat being dragged backwards while it clawed the ground,' Ross said. Once on the back of the truck it was taken back to Melbourne, where it was stored for a few years. Ross toyed with the decision to eventually restore it but decided to move the LE coupe onto another enthusiast, one with the dream of owning one of these limited edition coupes. ∎

TOP LEFT This LE sat idle in a driveway in Victoria for a decade.
ABOVE Lots of TLC, including de-moulding the interior, breathed new life into the coupe.

THE LONE RANGER

This is the story of how Indiana Dave unearthed a cracker of a barn find. His discovery turned out to be a low-mile, one-owner 1974 Valiant VJ Ranger covered in dust that had been tucked away in a weathered old farm shed for more than 15 years.

Indiana Dave, from Boorowa in New South Wales was told by his neighbour a couple of years ago about an old car in a shed, so he went to have a closer look. When Dave pulled up and saw a rotting old shed his heart began to beat faster, and he could see part of a car through the missing door planks. As he slowly pulled open the shed door, a huge smile broke across his face: in the shed lay a lone Ranger covered in a thick layer of dust and dirt.

When Dave enquired about the price he was disheartened, as it was a great car but not for the sort of money that was being asked. Sometime later he heard that the property with the old Ranger on it was for sale. Potential buyers inspected the property and some of them spotted the Ranger, but luckily for Dave nobody enquired about the car. However, he was worried that someone would pull bits off it. As the months passed, he often wondered if the Ranger was still in the shed.

One day while Indiana Dave was working on his truck a ute pulled up. The driver introduced himself

as Greg Edgerton and said he was one of the owners of Red Hill, the same property that housed the lone Ranger. Greg had come to ask Dave to transport some farm machinery to his new property, so Dave casually asked if the Valiant Ranger was still in the shed. Indiana Dave already had quite a collection of cars, but he decided he couldn't let the Ranger go again. A deal was negotiated, Greg got his machinery moved and Dave got the Ranger.

Over time Dave has been able to piece together the history of the Ranger, which is a well-preserved

> *Joyce was a very short lady who had to sit on a pillow so she could see over the steering wheel.*

time capsule.

Greg Edgerton's uncle Lyndon and his wife Joyce ran the family property of Red Hill. They drove around in an old work ute but planned to purchase a sedan for Joyce. As 1975 was rumoured to be a good year for wool prices, they decided to splurge and buy themselves a new one. On 4 April they drove to Kingsway Motors Chrysler in Goulburn, where they spotted a VJ Ranger sedan with just 30 kilometres on the odometer. As the VJ was a demonstrator,

the ownership document was labelled 'CAL Fleet', which stands for Chrysler Australia Limited. Joyce now had a brand new, comfortable car to drive.

With the ute carrying out the bulk of the driving duties, the Ranger didn't clock up many kilometres. Joyce was a very short lady who had to sit on a pillow so she could see over the steering wheel. This pillow was still in the car when it was pulled out of the shed. The Edgertons were very religious and attended regular church services. Joyce would usually drive the car to church, and locals recalled that she would have to do a lap of the block in order to come down the main street and park on the roadway in front of the church. The Ranger, which

is the size of a tank by today's standards, didn't have power steering and Joyce had trouble manoeuvring it around the church car park; it was easier to drive it around the block first.

Lyndon passed away in 1997 aged 84 years, and Joyce passed away the following year at the age of 79. She kept driving the Ranger right up until six months before she died. The couple had no children, so the property and the Ranger were passed on to the Edgerton's remaining family, which is how

TOP Note the Ranger's exterior windscreen sun visor.
ABOVE Brown vinyl interior and yellow paint – so very 1970s.

Greg ended up with the job of clearing the property of the farm machinery and of course the Ranger.

Dave was amazed at the condition of the car when he first discovered it. The shed had kept the rain and hot sun out, but there was a mountain of dust and dirt on and throughout the car. The condition of the interior struck him immediately: he thought it was simply superb, with no rips or tears whatsoever. The dash pad was in perfect condition and the carpets still looked new. When Dave wiped the dust off the instrument lens his eyes were instantly drawn to the odometer, which showed a mere 40,290 kilometres. He worked out that the old Ranger had travelled about 1,000 kilometres per year, which is super-low mileage for a 38-year-old car. It's no wonder the vehicle was in such good condition.

Dave brought his family with him to the shed where the lone Ranger lay entombed. He armed himself with two cameras so he could capture plenty of photographs to document his find. He brought a jerry can of fresh fuel, a charged battery, a set of jumper leads (just in case), a tow strap and an air compressor to pump up the flat tyres. He checked the oil and water levels and fitted the freshly charged battery. He was about to top up the fuel tank when he noticed that the petrol gauge was showing it as being half full. He decided to try to run the car on the fuel that was in the tank, figuring it might still be the higher octane leaded variety, or 'super' as it was known then, which was phased out in Australia by 2002.

Dave crossed his fingers and turned the key. Instantly the engine cranked over but protested at being disturbed from its long sleep. It gave a few coughs but wouldn't start. He gave it another go, and this time it started and ran for a few seconds before cutting out. Dave poured some fresh petrol into the carburettor and tried one more time. He turned the key again, whispered the bush mechanic's prayer – 'Come on: start, ya bastard' – and then she fired up and kept running. He revved it ever so slightly and took in the unmistakeable sound of the Hemi 265cid

> *This is quite incredible for a car that spent 23 years in rural New South Wales, where almost all the roads it travelled on were dirt and gravel!*

humming away. She was alive, and Indiana Dave's smile stretched from ear to ear!

Surprisingly, after all the years there was still a brake pedal. The old Ranger was driven back to Dave's home after a brief safety check. During the drive Dave noticed how smoothly the car ran, but he could the feel the flat spots on the tyres where they had squared off from sitting around for so long.

Unfortunately, he also noticed the temperature gauge beginning to creep up past halfway. He made it home just as the needle had edged its way into the red. That was close, he thought. A mental note was made to recheck the cooling system. Dave said that getting the Ranger home on a trailer would've been a better way to go, but as he had only 4 kilometres to cover he couldn't resist the itch to drive his Survivor home.

It took Dave three full days to clean up the Ranger. He degreased the engine and pressure washed the duco, followed by more high-pressure washing and then a hand sponge wash. Finally, he buffed it to within an inch of its life. Dave then set about cleaning the interior. While scrubbing away, he was transfixed for a moment when he noticed Joyce's finger marks on the sun visor where she would have pulled it down to shield her eyes from the piercing sun.

The overheating problem was next on the list. Inspecting the thermostat housing, Dave found that it was blocked solid: the thermostat had completely disintegrated. He thoroughly flushed out the cooling system, checked the carburettor and spark plugs and changed the oil and the oil filter. He noticed that it still had its original windscreen, as the stock number sticker was still there. This is quite incredible for a car that spent 23 years in rural New South Wales, where almost all the roads it travelled on were dirt and gravel!

Dave found the owner's manual and service books in the glovebox along with a box of Butter-Menthol and Irish Moss throat lozenges, and of course the pillow that Joyce sat on when she drove. In the boot sat a beautifully preserved original factory spare tyre that had obviously never been used. Sitting on top of the spare was a brand new spare fanbelt still in its original packaging. A curious item was a multicoloured foam drink container with a green cup. Many would remember these containers, as they were very popular in the 1970s. Dave also discovered a rat's nest in the passenger side front wheel arch. Thankfully they hadn't chewed through the brake lines or gotten into the interior. After much cleaning and polishing, Dave's once diamond in the rough shone as bright as the day it was sold new. This Ranger was certainly well maintained during its life and is an exceptional example of a Survivor. ■

LEFT Remarkably, the Ranger fired up and new owner Dave was able to drive it home, rat's nest in the front passenger side wheel well and all.

BATHURST-SPEC COBRA

The car featured here is not only a pucker Bathurst-spec Cobra, fitted with the 351 cubic inch V8 engine mated to the robust Borg Warner four-speed transmission, it is also the last of the 30 that were made. In fact, Cobra No. 31 is the very last race-homologated car produced by the Ford Motor Company. It was sold through the Mount Barker Motor Company and was originally purchased by R.A. Hosking from Glenelg, South Australia in January 1979. As it turned out another person, Rhett Polley, had made their way up to take a look at the car only to be told that the car had just been sold.

Five years later, when Rhett was working in Mildura, he saw an XC Cobra being put up on display ramps for sale at a local Ford dealer. Incredibly, he discovered this was the very same car, now with 24,000 kilometres on the odometer. After taking the car for a spin, he purchased it then and there. Interestingly, the second-hand value of the car had risen from the new price of $11,166 to $14,700. Rhett was now the second owner, the first apparently selling the car due to a loss of licence.

> *The value of the car had risen from the new price of $11,166 to $14,700.*

Rhett damaged his spine in 1985 and the resulting nerve damage meant he was no longer physically able to drive the four-speed manual Cobra, so regrettably he had to hang up the keys in 1995. The car sat forlornly in his carport for the next 21 years, slowly gaining the patina of time until he finally conceded that the car was never likely to get recommissioned during his ownership.

Mark Negri discovered the car unexpectedly. He was passing time on Facebook at a pub in Streaky Bay, South Australia after losing a front wheel on his LandCruiser while travelling home to Perth from a Christmas holiday. He quickly organised someone to inspect the long-hibernating Cobra on his behalf and a deal was struck.

Mark remembers his dad taking him as a kid to a showroom to look at a Cobra and at one point he owned Cobra No. 62, so it was in the blood. In fact, he recently sold a Red Pepper XA GT hardtop to make room for his new purchase.

LEFT Parked in a carport in 1995, there it stayed for the next 21 years!
ABOVE Genuine 1978 Bathurst alloy Globe wheels still remain with this Cobra.

By way of background, of the 400 Cobras built the first 200 had the 5.8 litre V8 and the second 200 were fitted with the 4.9 litre V8. The exceptions were build No. 1, which was fitted with a 4.9 litre V8, and build No, 351, which rather appropriately was fitted with the same number of cubic inches as its numeric designation.

With Mark's newly acquired Cobra, beneath the tree detritus and dust the aggressive paint scheme of Sno White and Bold Blue is still striking. Surface rust has started to creep from areas of steel where the paint has been chipped away by road debris and from thinly painted factory edges such as around the bonnet scoop cut-out. Flat tyres and corroded alloys and the fine crazing covering much of the paint detract

> *It is a car that could well get awards in a preservation-class concours.*

from what, with a thorough detail, is a car that could well get awards in a preservation-class concours.

Lifting the bonnet reveals an extra oil cooler, twin thermo fans and a strut brace unique to Bathurst-spec cars, and factory markings such as the '31' scribbled on the underside of the scoop. The interior is complete bar the non-original steering wheel, and will no doubt scrub up to as new with a little elbow grease. The odometer

within the comprehensive instrument cluster now displays a genuine 57,426 kilometres.

Mark had the car being recommissioned in South Australia with the intention of preserving its Survivor car status. He has also been in contact with the original owner, who was really keen to see the car again. Mark had plans to swing past his place before taking the car back home to the west. ■

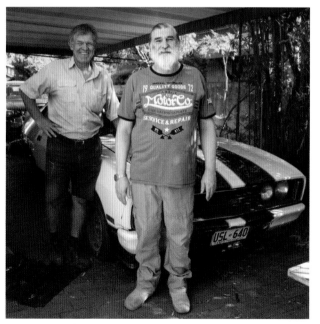

LEFT Bingo! The ID tags match the VIN and the engine number.
RIGHT The car's second owner Rhett (in front) with Ken, who was sent to inspect it on behalf of the new owner, Mark.

OLD WARRIOR

The only way to find old cars is to drive an old car and talk to old people. Motoring historian and part-time car hunter Ross Vasse was in Gippsland, Victoria in an old Falcon GT and stopped for morning tea in the main street of a small town when he was approached by a local, Santo. One thing led to another, and the next thing Ross knew he was on a dirt road looking for an old Monaro . . .

Any good car hunter knows that when you get a lead that's hotter than a hooker's doorknob on dollar night you leave no stone unturned. Santo called the owner to ask if Ross could come to look at the car: 'Hi Paul, I got a bloke here who wants to come and take some photos of the cars.'

'Yeah, no worries, mate. I'm up the back milking cows, but have them go to the back shed and meet me there.'

Upon arriving, Ross spotted the Monaro under a lean-to on the property and Paul approaching on his tractor. 'G'day, Santo told me you were coming. The calves are in the back shed, so take as many photos as you want.'

'Pardon? Umm, calves? I'm here to see the car – the old Monaro over there.'

'Oh, cars! I thought Santo said you wanted to take photos of the calves. It did seem odd,' he said, shaking his head and muttering. 'That Santo . . . Yeah, no worries, go for your life.'

Paul has been a dairy farmer all his life and had owned the HX Monaro GTS since he was 16 years old. He bought it in 1981 from the Pink Pig used car yard in Morwell, Victoria for $5,800, showing 48,000 kilometres on the clock.

'I was in Morwell driving around with mates and spotted the Monaro,' Paul said, 'so I stopped and made a deal to buy it.' The Monaro looked the goods on the used car lot, and being a four-on-the-floor suited Paul. 'It only had a 253 in it, but later I swapped it out for a 308 with a big cam, roller rockers, Edelbrock manifold and extractors that had 500 hp.'

TOP Rats, mice and spiders made their home in the Monaro when it was retired to the farm.
LEFT Even the cows have taken a liking to the Monaro's door – or is that a disliking?

After work on a Friday or Saturday night, Paul would hoon around with his mates looking for girls and some street-racing action. 'I remember blowing away Ken Anderson's white XY GT from a standing start. It was a long straight and I beat him in top gear,' Paul said of his illegal drag-racing days. 'One night I raced a gold VC Commodore, and he whipped my arse. I was pissed off. The next day I went to my brother-in-law's workshop and we re-done the heads and added a bigger cam,' he recounted.

'Another night we were on our way into Melbourne to the Cindi Lauper concert for some fun with the girls when this guy in a red XB GT lined us up on the freeway for a rolling start. The Monaro blew his doors off, and one of my female passengers stuck her arm out the window to give him the finger. But my fondest memory was getting my first shag in the back of the Monaro with a girl called Maria.

'One night, a mate and I took the Monaro to Warragul for dinner, and a bloke says, "That looks like my old car!"' He told Paul, 'If I didn't have four kids at the time I'd never have sold it!'

> *'If I didn't have four kids at the time I'd never have sold it!'*

Paul seems to have lived the good old days well, and the old warrior, the Cotillion White Monaro, was parked up and last registered in 1997. Paul added personal number plates, PP-307, but his biggest regret was adding the pop-up sunroof. 'They were the in thing back then,' he said. The old Monaro is now covered in dust and cobwebs.

Paul has a framed photo of the Monaro back in its heyday looking sharp with a set of Cragar mags. As for whether or not the Monaro will ever be for sale – well, cockies usually don't sell anything. 'I get tanker trucks picking up milk and dropping

TOP LEFT After being beaten in a race with a VC Commodore the engine received a bigger cam and had the heads redone.
BOTTOM LEFT Last registered in 1997.

off fuel all time. Just about every new driver asks me, "How much do you want for the old Holden?" and I tell them, "She's not for sale."' ■

CROWN JEWEL

Thirty-six years is a very long time between drinks for a car not to have been started. Since 1985, to be exact. Coincidentally, this Mazda RX-4's last drink was of the leaded fuel known as 'super', which had remained in the tank ever since. Super petrol doesn't go off like today's fuel, which has a limited shelf life. In 2021 this 1974 Mazda RX-4 13B Series 2 Hardtop came to life again when she fired up first go.

Rod Luckett was nobody's fool; he knew what he had. Such was the interest in his car that he had a stack of notes with people's names and numbers he'd kept over the years. His Mazda RX-4 had been up on bricks for decades, parked under the large carport adjoining the heritage-listed Moama post office building where Rod lived. Rod wasn't a hoarder per se, but he wasn't akin to letting things go either. He preferred to put them away for a rainy day, such as his boat, dune buggy, an old caravan and his Toyota Coaster bus converted to a camper.

Ross Vasse was on a family vacation one Easter. 'We had just crossed the Murray River and turned right towards the holiday park,' Ross said, 'when my eye caught something with round headlights.' Not one to doubt his intuition, he did a U-turn to appease his curiosity. 'I could see in the semi-darkness of the enclosure, behind two gates

padlocked with a thick chain, an old Japanese car: a Mazda RX-4! Blimey, a coupe at that! I put a note in the letterbox to express my interest.

'Every day while on holidays I'd take my morning walk in the direction of the Mazda in the hope someone was home. On the second-last day before we were due to go home an old bloke was unlocking the gate to enter.' When Ross asked the bloke, Rod Luckett, about the car he said: 'If you're going to ask me if it's for sale, it's not.' Ross respected the fact that the owner didn't want to sell the car but asked if he could leave his number. Rod said: 'Sure, I'll add it to the pile I already have.'

As luck would have it, Ross bumped into Rod at the local RSL that evening. They chatted, with Rod talking about owning the Moama post office and the recent spate of burglaries that had resulted in the locked gates. The RX-4 wasn't discussed.

The next day as they were leaving, Ross saw Rod out the front of his home and jumped out to ask if he could have a quick look at the Mazda and take a few photos. He was impressed with the originality, although the Mazda had seen better days. 'The front seats were unbolted, as Rod had removed the CB radio and coaxial cabling, but the interior condition attested to the original mileage of 37,000 miles.

'I've always had a soft spot for the RX-4 ever since a mate had one we painted Vermilion Fire in enamel with a Little Beaver when we were 18 years old,' Ross reminisced. 'We painted it outside on a cold day, and you wouldn't believe the dust particles and orange peel in the paintwork! It was terrible up close, but looked good from far.'

Every year when Ross headed up to the river he'd stop in to say hello to Rod. Rod's knees needed an operation and he ended up having to use a walking frame. 'One day quite a few years later I saw Rod struggling up his driveway,' Ross said. 'He told me that he'd had two lots of bad news from his doctor.' Ross never asked Rod about selling the Mazda again.

In late 2018, Ross received a letter he had sent to Rod with 'Return to sender' on the envelope. Inside was a handwritten courtesy card from the New South Wales State Trustees Department informing him that Rod Luckett had passed away.

Ross called family member Denise to offer his condolences, then asked what had happened to Rod's estate. 'I told Denise there was a car I was interested in,' Ross explained. 'She told me it was complicated due to having to work with the Victorian state trustee, but that she'd keep me updated via email. She was not aware of the Mazda as it wasn't on the asset register, so I sent her the photos. She said she'd sent a representative to check if the car was still there.' Ross waited anxiously for a week or so before receiving an email from Denise

stating the Mazda was still there and was now on the asset register, but it would take some time to sort out the estate.

'Quite some time passed, and every time I remembered it I'd flick an email to Denise. Then one day I received a reply that the estate had settled, and I was to submit a tender,' Ross continued. 'I really wanted that car: where was I going to find another unrestored RX-4 coupe? So I put in a tender well above what the market value was and a few days later received an email saying I had been successful!'

One of Rod's family members, Wayne, had the Mazda ready for the tow truck with the tyres

LEFT It's just our two cents' worth, but this RX-4 would be widely lusted after.
BELOW It wasn't pretty, but the Mazda started up A-okay..

technician when it comes to old cars – and together with Yogi we attempted to start her,' Ross retold of the nail-biting experience.

'We had a can of Start YaBastard, and surprisingly the super petrol in the tank was still good. When she fired she ran perfectly, albeit with a ton of white smoke bellowing out the exhaust. This was because of all the lubricant squirted inside the ports, but in truth I was worried when it looked like a long white cloud drifting over the neighbour's house. I feared a rebuild was in hand.

'Then, after about three minutes of revving at 5,000 rpm, the exhaust came as clean as a whistle, idling perfectly afterwards,' Ross said with delight.

Admittedly, the carbie needed a rebuild afterwards and the brakes and clutch needed overhauling. On its initial short but spirited shake-down road test, everything worked perfectly. Ross said: 'If you've never driven a rotary, it's a weird sensation where the engine produces power without the resistance you'd experience in a regular piston motor.'

pumped up. 'Wayne said the front brakes were seized on, and he had to cut the brake lines,' Ross said. 'I drove up from Melbourne that morning to meet Wayne and to watch it get loaded. If it wasn't for my mate Yogi Bear, who came with me, I'd have missed the boot rack and CB aerial he spotted that were tucked away in the garage rafters.'

> *Ross spent quite a few hours giving the RX-4 hardtop a spruce up.*

Starting the Mazda involved removing the spark plugs, priming the ports and spinning the motor over daily for a few days. When the day came to get her going, Ross was aware it could go either way and was prepared for the worst: an engine rebuild. 'I've known Chris for 30 years – he's a master

Ross spent quite a few hours giving the RX-4 hardtop a spruce up, buffing the aged paintwork, which appears to have had an external repaint in factory Jewel Green. The white vinyl roof was given some shoe polish treatment, which resulted in a well-deserved sheen. The saddle interior with its overhead cockpit-style console was considered to be in great condition, with only minor wear and tear consistent with the relatively low odometer reading. 'When I removed the rear number plate to clean in behind the panel, I noticed a key that was secured by the screw. This was where Rod kept it, just in case.'

Ross changed the wheels back to the original from the Minilites it wore. So original was this RX-4, the factory-fitted windscreen had the aerial imbedded in the glass. 'Sure she's got a few battle scars and she's showing her age, but it's still one of the most original Survivor RX-4s I've ever seen,' Ross said. 'And the quirky colour combo and vinyl roof just screams the 1970s!' ∎

ABOVE Every young bloke's dream car, white vinyl roof and all.
BELOW The Mazda was fitted with some spiffy 1970s accessories.

THIS VEHICLE WAS MANUFACTUR
GENERAL MOTORS HOLDEN'S PTY.
TO COMPLY WITH AUSTRALIAN DESIGN

2,3,4,5A,7,10A,15,2

HOLDEN

LC TORANA SEDAN 2 DOO

3/71   LC 25

6 VW   183   SEAT
THIS PLATE IS AFFIXED WITH THE APP
AUSTRALIAN MOTOR VEHICLE CERTIFIC

GENERAL MOTORS - HOLDEN'S
BODY   IDENTIFICA
CORRESPONDENCE MUST BEAR THES
MODEL LC 8291
BODY NO 928-A
TRIM   18 3-40
PAINT   568 237
TOP
MADE IN AUSTRALIA

GENERAL MOTORS HOLDENS PTY

82911 LC 1704

PART II:
slumbering

GOOD BONES

Flash hero colours on new cars were introduced in the late 1960s and continued on until the mid-1970s, when things started to become bland again. Each manufacturer – especially the big three – wanted their cars to stand out from the crowd, and Holden went on the offensive with bright hues that could burn the retina off your eyes.

One of those colours was bright green, or Lina Mint, best remembered for its use on Torana XU-1s like the dusty muscle car here, so it's ironic that the owner of this 1971 Holden LC Torana GTR XU-1 likes to fly under the radar when it comes to others knowing what he's got tucked away.

By pure chance, Ross Vasse learned of the Torana owner's small collection of desirable cars when someone whispered, 'You should see what this bloke has out the back of town,' and like a rabbit down a hole he was on his front door in a shot. Although the car owner, Bruce, was a little on the back foot when he first answered the door, he soon realised Ross was a genuine classic car enthusiast by the classic he had pulled up in: a bummed-out Red Pepper XA GT that had trekked across the outback.

After the usual pleasantries Ross got down to the reason why he was there. Bruce said 'Follow me' and walked around to the back of the property into an old shed that had seen better days. With a nod of his head and an 'In here,' he motioned for Ross to enter as he held the door open.

The Lina Mint GTR XU-1 was parked on blocks right at the back. Ross also noticed a Calypso Green XA GT project car tucked away in the corner, along with bits and bobs such as a vintage monkey bike, an R series Valiant and even a four-barrel inlet manifold from a Hemi Pacer! As you can imagine, Bruce was a bit of a hoarder. He likes old stuff, stuff he grew up with. Stuff like muscle cars in bright colours. Ross figured he was partial to green.

'I found the old Torana back in 1993. In fact, it found me,' Bruce related. 'Back then I had a workshop at the back of a spare parts shop, and I saw the owner park it

out front. I knew it was genuine straight away.' Quick as a wink, Bruce approached the driver to ask if he'd consider selling. 'She was a little banged up around the edges, but I was interested,' Bruce continued. 'I said: "Would you take fifteen hundred for her?"'

'Nah, mate,' came the reply. 'I wouldn't take anything under $1,800 for it.'

Bruce smiled like a rat with a gold tooth as he retold the story, knowing what these things are fetching today. 'I drove it for a month or so until the rego ran out. It has sat there ever since. The guy I bought it from only had it 12 months, and it had originally come from Port Augusta. A mob in Port Augusta flared the guards, which I found out when I bumped into a bloke years later who said he did it,' Bruce said, 'but I got a pair of new old stock guards with it, which I plan to put on.'

This XU-1 was originally built in March 1971 at the Elizabeth General Motors-Holden assembly plant in South Australia and fitted with a 186Xci triple carbed red motor, four-on the floor, slippery rear end and a long-range fuel tank to ensure it got to its destination, fast. GTR XU-1 Toranas took over

from the GTS Monaros as Holden's race cars of choice in the eternal battle with the old enemy at Bathurst; they were the David to Ford's Goliath. The LC model bagged many victories on the tighter twisty circuits, particularly in the hands of Colin Bond. In 1970 the Holden Dealer Team's racing Toranas were painted Yellow Dolly and Lina Mint, just like Bruce's machine.

In 1972, Peter Brock ensured the XU-1 nameplate's fame by winning the Hardie-Ferodo

500 at Mount Panorama in the later LJ model. There were 1,397 GTR XU-1s built between 1970 and 1971. For peace of mind, Bruce had removed all three ID tags for safekeeping.

Bruce's game plan is to restore the pocket rocket to stock standard. He says he'll have the flares removed and get an original spec engine back in it. 'She might be banged up, but she's got good bones.' Bruce is a doer, not a gunna, and he started putting aside $100 a week into a special fund to pay for restoring this old girl. After this he'll get on to fixing up that old XA GT in the corner, which has also been in dry storage for decades. ■

BOTTOM LEFT You don't see many vintage monkey bikes these days.
CENTRE LEFT Original SA number plates have stayed with the Torana for its life..

THE CHICKEN COUPE

Over the years many people had heard about or even seen the odd photo of the chicken coupe, a Ford Falcon XA GT hardtop that had been parked for decades inside, well, a chicken coop. All kinds of gossip and hearsay had been said about its origins and how it came to be behind the chicken wire. Here is the real story behind the chicken coupe and its humble owner, someone passionate about the car despite its sad condition.

'As soon as I saw it I had to have it!' Gordon recalled from his home in Queensland. 'I was 31 years old and a Telecom technical officer, driving a satin red XP Falcon. Like everyone else, I was expecting the Phase IV to be released in a hardtop; I couldn't wait! Then the Super Car scare hits the front page of newspapers, claiming every young bloke would jump behind the wheel and instantly wrap themselves around a telegraph pole at 160 miles per hour!

'But then I heard about a special GT with GT-HO options. Ford was getting rid of all the Phase IV parts under the radar, and I wanted one. I'd seen the manager of Metro Ford driving this incredible-looking XA GT hardtop. The manager had parked the hardtop in the middle of the showroom floor and it drew everyone like moths to a flame.'

Metro Ford, located at Spring Hill in Brisbane, was known as the 'big guys': 'That's what they called themselves back then,' Gordon said. The manager had been using the big Falcon every night to commute home, which drummed up sales with increased foot traffic to the showroom. As a demo, it had a few hundred miles on the clock up until that time. 'The moment I realised it was one of the specials, my heart raced. I could have bought a GT-HO Phase III for less but I wanted the XA, so I got a $1,000 trade-in on the XP and handed out around $7,000 for the hardtop.'

From 1974 onwards Gordon was the first registered owner of the chicken coupe. 'I drove it everywhere. If I was at work I parked it down the back under a shady tree.' Gordon had certainly come a long way since stepping up from a VW Beetle as his first car, then from the XP to the XA.

Gordon was born in 1942 in the same month his regular production option (RPO) was built. After just one year of ownership, he used his GT as his wedding car. Life moved quickly, encompassing a wife, kids and work. 'I worked down at Batlow for a time and remember pulling over for coffee. It was lightly snowing and the temperature change blew the ceramic water pump seal, so I had to stop at

LEFT Surrounded by period soft drink cans, this old hardtop yearns to return to the road one day. BOTTOM RIGHT The engine remains factory spec.

every gully, creek and dam to top up the radiator. I had water in a bucket pouring it in every chance I got, all the way home!'

In 1988 Australian insurance premiums skyrocketed, especially if you owned a high-performance vehicle. 'I just couldn't afford the insurance premium for the GT,' Gordon recalled, 'so I parked it. I always intended to get it back on the road but time moved on very quickly.'

Gordon's RPO hardtop is painted in rare MacRobertson's Old Gold, a rich orange hue that is the corporate colour of confectionery company MacRobertson's, and was fully optioned with power steering, integrated air, power windows, two-piece sports road wheels, eight-track radio/

stereo tape player, front and rear spoilers, factory-fitted rear louvre and tinted side glass. Topping off these options was the coveted RPO 83, which incorporated components from the stillborn GT-HO Phase IV parts bin.

Fast forward some three decades, and the rumours about this car had firmed Ford hardtop tragic Troy Postle's resolve to find it and unlock its story. 'I knew about the XA GT RP0 83, but not its exact location,' Troy, from Queensland, said. 'When I had heard rumours about it being sold, I had to know for sure. So I thought: *I'm going to find it.*

'I asked around and narrowed the search. The GT RPO 83 had been documented before but its exact location was kept a secret, and for good reason. It's one of only two in this colour, and adding to its uniqueness is that only 120 XA GT RPO 83s were ever produced. I remember when I spotted the unmistakable XA GT bonnet sticking its nose out

from under the small corrugated shed, which was surrounded by chicken wire. I parked my own XA GT hardtop to show I was an enthusiast and then knocked on the door a couple of times.'

'Yeah?' Gordon said, poking his head out of the front window and studying Troy with a curious eye.

'That's my XA GT hardtop out front,' Troy indicated with a lazy thumb over his shoulder. 'I'd love to talk to you about your hardtop.'

Gordon inspected Troy's immaculate XA GT hardtop then led Troy to his own pride and joy. 'I've owned it since new. People keep pestering me to sell it to them. I reckon I've had over 500 offers! One bloke even offered to take it off my hands for nothing! I suppose you want to buy it too?'

Troy smiled back. 'No, Gordon, I just love Fords, and especially hardtops!'

Gordon nodded, and looked around his quiet property then back at Troy. 'Everyone keeps telling

me what I should be doing with it. I've thought about restoring it but then all the memories would be washed away.'

Troy nodded and studied the rare car behind the chicken wire, which stared back with one broken driving light lens and the other dull from sun fade. Looking sad, the old Falcon's wings had truly been clipped over time. Surrounded by old soft drink cans and bottles, its tyres sat deflated on American alloy racing rims that had long ago been swapped over from the factory option 52 mags. There was rust in the bonnet, along the A pillar and around the boot, and the big Falcon's panels were dented on the driver's side door and quarter. The rear valance panel was jutting out on the left from being caught on something.

Looking beyond the dust and cobwebs, this RPO was graced with unique dealer-fitted sidewinder

TOP LEFT Rats have had a party in the big Ford's interior.
ABOVE This XA GT cuts a sad figure now but lived a good early life.

stripes, which start at the GT 351 badge at the fenders and sweep over its flanks at the rear. The mark of a hardtop with good bones is to find it still fitted with the original stainless wheel arch moulds, and to

its credit they're still fitted on this GT – even the left-hand rear one, which is usually the first to go from accident damage.

Opening the door, Troy was met with the stench of a rat party that had been going on for years. Gordon remarked, 'The rats have gotten in there and chewed the wiring. They have gotten into my other car too.' Inside everything was pretty much standard; even the eight-track stereo had been frozen in time with Elvis' *Rock 'N' On* hits in the tape deck.

The front passenger seat was no longer in the car. 'The seat rail had broken, and my passenger would almost fall into the back seat on acceleration so I took the seat out,' Gordon said. His work mates thought this was hilarious, and joked that he looked like a chauffeur. The front seat and the factory rear louvre had been put away for safekeeping. This RPO

> " *This RPO was graced with unique dealer-fitted sidewinder stripes.*

was upgraded at Metro Ford with orange-flavoured Hawaiian cloth inserts, which is another unique day two mod that sets this car apart from others. Fast glass is factory fitted.

The engine bay was as close to bog stock as you'd expect, with the big 351cid Cleveland V8 and its 4V big port heads nestled nicely within. 'The heads have never been off,' Gordon said. Even the original HM headers are still fitted. The ID tags have never been removed, and wiping away the dust reveals the paint code Y157: MacRoberston's Old Gold. Underneath, the sturdy nine-inch diff was covered in grease and grime, but Gordon stated she had a genuine Detroit Locker unit.

The hardtop had been parked up for over 30 years, near double the time it had spent on the road beforehand. Since 1988 Gordon had been driving a HQ that is fitted with a 253cid V8, but that too has been parked under a tree for ages. 'They reckon the [XA] needs this and that, that it should be tucked away so no one will see it. This car is my memories; if I sold it I would be selling part of my family. It's staying where it is. Anyway, if I moved it away or covered it up no one would pop in for a chat, which I don't mind on the odd occasion.'

It was a privilege for Troy to get a closer look at the chicken coupe. He developed a friendship with Gordon, and felt honoured that he'd been able to share the real story behind this special car. 'To dispel the rumour that the shed the car was in was once a chicken coop and that chickens lived in the shed with the RPO: that was never the case,' Troy revealed. 'It was only called the chicken coupe because Gordon put chicken wire across the front of the shed to keep the homing pigeons out, as they would poop on the car when nesting in the rafters.' ■

BELOW Long-time owner Gordon kept the car for sentimental reasons. 'This car is my memories,' he declared. Sadly, since this story was documented Gordon has passed away.

TARGA FLORIO FIND

Alan MacTavish, from Forestville in Sydney, knows his Leyland products as he is an ex-BMC engineer. He played a part in the P76 pre-production stage in the early 1970s but had moved on when the P76 was released in 1973. He was after a good set of wheels at the beginning of the 1980s, his prerequisites being that it had to be a BMC product and have a V8 under the bonnet so he could work on it. The Leyland P76 V8 certainly fit the bill!

When the P76 was first released it won *Wheels* car of the year for 1973. Sadly, this didn't reverberate with the general public, as it suffered quality-control issues due to industrial disputes and insufficient development funding by Leyland, and it also had the bad luck of landing smack bang in the middle of the 1973 oil crisis. The controversial European styling was penned by Giovanni Michelotti, whose portfolio included designs for Ferrari, Maserati, BMW and Triumph, but it was looked upon as being weird looking and many Australian car buyers didn't connect with it. Unfortunately for the marque it was unfairly labelled a lemon, which resulted in suffering sales.

The P76's body was strong and light and the steering nimble thanks to the rack and pinion steering and MacPherson strut front suspension, and it had ample passenger and boot space. The engine options included the 2.6 litre 6-cylinder, but the one to go for was the light, all-aluminium 4.4 litre V8, which produced a respectable amount of power. Other innovative features were a front-hinged bonnet, coil-sprung rear end, glued-in windscreen and concealed windscreen wipers. It also had front disc brakes and a limited slip differential as standard features across the whole range.

The lemon tag stuck and many P76s suffered from neglect. However, some Leylands were cherished and well looked after by a solid base of P76 followers who realised that, given time and some minor improvements, it would've been a real contender in the big Aussie sedan market.

Alan MacTavish eventually tracked down a special P76, a limited edition Targa Florio model in Nutmeg, from used car dealer Valley Car Sales in

Seaforth in November 1983. He always considered the Targa Florio, named after a P76's stage win in the 1974 World Cup Rally, to be a special car. The Florio had originally been purchased on 8 November 1974 from Leyland Australia in Wentworthville and wore the registration number HBB-697. In 1984

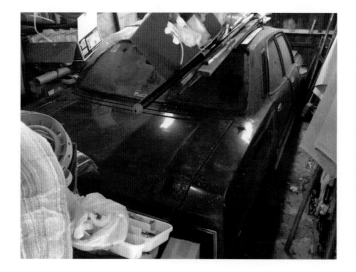

the Targa had some repairs carried out on its LSD differential that totalled $585, quite a hefty sum then. Over the next few years Alan did a lot of tinkering to the motor, including an engine rebuild.

By 1988 the body was starting to look a bit tired and rough. Alan purchased a clean and straight 1974 Leyland P76 Executive from Ian Waddell, who ran a BMC/Leyland parts supply business in Dural, the plan being to drop the good motor into the tidy Executive and then sell the Targa with the old Executive motor. In 1990 Alan made some space and hired an engine hoist to swap the

'The process was a lot more involved than I first thought.'

V8s over. He later admitted, 'The process was a lot more involved than I first thought.'

The following year, Alan abandoned the plan. The Targa was driven a little between 1983 and 1990 and the Executive was only ever driven home from the car yard. Its registration expired in 1989 and was never renewed. No one else in the family was interested in Alan's P76s but he wouldn't consider selling them, as prices in the early 1990s were very low.

Family commitments meant Alan's plans for the cars never came to fruition, and he finally decided he could no longer keep the P76s. Although his original plan never came off, it certainly saved the

LEFT AND ABOVE P76s don't get a lot of respect, especially brown ones. However, they have a special place in Australia's proud history of car manufacturing.

P76s. The Targa is still in very good condition with its matching numbers engine, as is the Executive. With some work and a minimum of hassle, both vehicles could be up and running. It's a win for both P76s, as they get to hang around and be admired by their new owners and other car lovers. ∎

SUBURBAN BARN FIND

arn finds are often urban myths, fanciful stories told by those with adventurous minds, but on very rare occasions those myths are proven to be true and are sometimes sitting right under our noses. How many times have you wondered what is behind that shed door? The suburban barn find: many car enthusiasts have dreamed of finding an old classic Survivor lying in wait, a gem in a shed locked away where nobody can find it, then a chance conversation or a throwaway line catches the attention of a car hunter. The suburban jungle is littered with garages and sheds, many appearing to have been inoperative long term. Often the sheds match the style and age of the houses they accompany, leading inquisitive passers-by to pose the question: what's in the shed?

Every now and then you've just got to be in the right place at the right time, and asking the right questions.

Behind the closed doors of a fairly regular-looking corrugated iron shed is what can only be described as an epic barn find: an original 1958 Holden FC Special. The FC Holden was a very significant chapter in the history pages for Holden. The 500,000th vehicle they built was an FC, at a time when they dominated the market. A staggering fact is that in 1958 Holden had 50 per cent of the market share, a very different number from what

they currently hold. There was also a strong demand for exports, and FC Holdens were supplied to more than 15 countries including South Africa, Fiji, Thailand and Singapore.

Clearly influenced by other General Motors models sold overseas, the FC had loads of chrome – particularly on the Special model. Lavish side panels and fins adorned the car, and the two-tone paintwork accentuated the curves and edges of the body and differentiated them from the regular model. The FC had many admirers, which is a testament to how popular this car has become with car enthusiasts across the country.

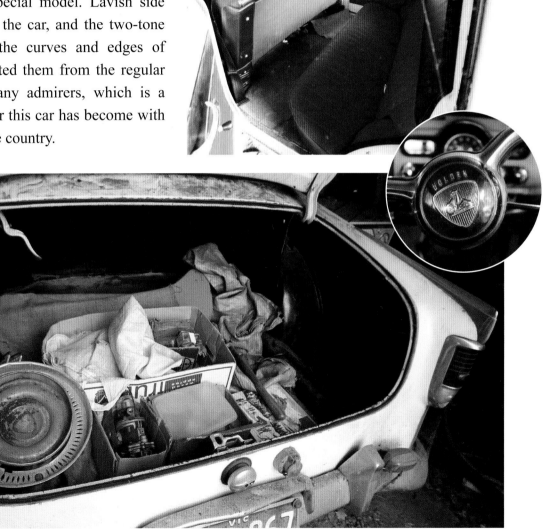

LEFT A humble sheet protects the duco.
BELOW A boot full of car parts in boxes warms the heart of any car enthusiast.

RIGHT The FC Special remains in the family of its original owners to be appreciated by new generations. It's been parked for over 25 years.

The discovery of this FC barn find stemmed from a chance conversation with Marcus Whelan, a car enthusiast who has grown up around performance cars. 'We've had an HX sedan in the family for a long time – it is a bit of a street machine,' he explained. 'I just mentioned that my grandmother had an old car in a shed, so we went to take a look.'

This FC Holden Special Survivor was bought as a gift for Edwin and Ethel Phillips in 1959. The Phillips family had helped support Edwin's sister Violet through some tough times, and to show her thanks once she got back on her feet Violet bought them this car. It was an ex-demo car from PS Carey Motors in Bacchus Marsh, Victoria and had very few miles on it when it was purchased. 'I have some great memories of Gramps and Nini's car,' Marcus said. 'I loved going to the tip with Gramps: I'd help him load up and then he'd let us sit in the trailer all the way there!'

For many years the trusty FC Special served as the family transport for the Phillips family, with daily duties to and from the shops as well as towing the caravan or trailer. 'As a kid it was always a novelty to be in the car with Gramps. We didn't wear seatbelts in the back – there wasn't any fitted!' Marcus recalled.

Edwin didn't drive the car much in the 1980s, and sadly passed away in 1988. Ethel continued paying the registration on the car until 1993, just in case someone needed to use the car. 'The funny thing is, Nini has never had a driver's licence. I'm not even sure she's ever driven the car.'

This special FC has been parked for more than 25 years, the flat tyres and spiderwebs testament to the sands of time that have blown by. Remarkably, the car is still in fairly good condition, as the earthern floor in the shed has protected it from the elements over the years. 'There are no plans for the car at this stage; it will continue to sit safely in Nini's shed out of harm's way until the family can work out the best way to appreciate the car,' Marcus stated.

This true one-owner barn find has sat quietly in suburbia covered up behind its corrugated shield, and there this Survivor will continue to sit, waiting for the right time to be revived by its family owners. ▪

CLAYTON'S JOHN GOSS SPECIAL

**M**any have said there are no barns in Australia; well, look again. Here we have a real barn with a real barn find hidden away inside in the form of an old, worn-out 1975 Ford Falcon 500 hardtop that has seen better days. Could this be the fabled prototype John Goss Special that was rumoured to have been built in Walnut Glow? It has all the hallmarks of it being this car, except one . . .

Purchased as a demonstrator model from Col Paige Ford in Melbourne's west in 1975 with around 1,500 hundred clicks, this car was ordered with option 90 – 'Delete Wax' – indicating it was built to order for a customer who ticked each specific option and as such would not have needed wax protection. It is not known how or why it ended up a demo model, but it is known that Theo van Gaans, a Polish immigrant and engineer by trade from Ballarat, came across the hardtop sitting on the showroom floor in Cowper Street, Footscray and instantly fell in love with it.

When he bought the big Falcon it had the appearance of a John Goss Special (JGS): the white-painted factory 12-slot wheels, single-headlight white grille, orange pinstripe, sports instrumentation, white vinyl trim, 302 V8 and four-on-the-floor, but it was painted Walnut Glow

over Polar White with chrome bumpers instead of the colour-coded bumpers usually found on a JGS. It is known that there were 700 JGS hardtops built, of which 371 were Apollo Blue and 329 Emerald Green. None were ever made in brown, although it has always been rumoured that the very first John Goss built, the prototype if you will, was built to Goss's own specifications and he chose Walnut Glow over Polar White.

Theo drove the Falcon as his daily driver up until the early 1980s, commuting to work around Ballarat where he worked for Bendix Mintex, the clutch and brake lining manufacturer, Timken Bearings and eventually McCain Foods as the production manager. Along the way he added the quad-headlamp grille and had the interior inserts changed to his favourite colour, a rich burgundy velour. Around this time Theo was given a company car so the old XB two-door was put aside, but he couldn't bring himself to part with it. Eventually, when Theo's son Greg turned 18, he was given the car as his runaround. Between 1982 and 1985 Greg commuted from Ballarat to Warrnambool, back in the day when the big Falcon hardtop was just another ordinary road car and one that was considered to be dated at that, like an old dinosaur. After providing reliable service for a number of years it was parked at Theo's mum's place back in Ballarat, where it stayed until his sad passing.

Greg inherited the brown hardtop. He said: 'I got it in around 2000, and had it brought to Adelaide. By then

LEFT Under lock and key, a special Falcon hardtop rests inside.
BELOW One day this 302cid V8 will fire up once more.
BOTTOM Red velour seat inserts!

the orange stripes had been removed. It never had the big 302 decals but rather the standard chrome badges,' Greg continued. 'Dad also added a twin exhaust system, and Aunger mag wheels along the way.'

Greg contacted a classic car magazine after reading an article on the Apollo Blue 'Survivor' John Goss Special. What piqued his interest were the comments about the rumoured brown car prototype. Thinking that it may well be his dad's old car, he emailed the vital numbers to the magazine, which they then checked with Ford Australia's production database.

This hardtop was built to every specification and option as the John Goss Special in October 1975, right in the middle of the second batch of John Goss Specials, which negates the chance of it being the prototype. However, someone knew enough back then to order a Falcon 500 to almost the exact specs as a genuine JGS. Remember that the Walnut Glow paintwork was already on the car when Theo first saw it in late 1975, and there's an old photo to support this. It even has the quarter-panel flutes that were

unique to the Falcon XB GT and John Goss Specials.

After being transported from Victoria to South Australia it was put away, and eventually made its way onto Greg's country retreat for safe storage. Rats, mice, spiders, slugs and snails have kept the big hardtop company, and it is now covered in cobwebs and pine needles. Showing just 99,823 kilometres on the clock, the matching numbers donk is still in it.

'I plan on getting the old dinosaur back on the road one day,' Greg said of his plans to restore the big Falcon. 'I owe it to Dad.' ▪

LEFT The Falcon fits snuggly inside a unique setting.
ABOVE The odometer reads 99,823 kilometres. When will she clock up 100 K?

BLACK BEAUTY

I t's amazing what you can stumble across in your travels – such as this rare Tuxedo Black 1980 Holden VC HDT Special Commodore that was discovered on a farm when Nathan decided to have a go at horse riding with his mate Dave. Everybody has a mate named Dave . . .

The lads rang around and found a horse trail riding business on the outskirts of Melbourne that was open and accommodated beginners. While travelling to their destination they almost missed the country driveway but luckily spotted a small, obscure sign stating 'Horse Riding Trail Rides Ahead – Turn Left in 200 metres'. Duly turning left, they drove up the long, dirt driveway over a slight hill towards a 1950s-style house hidden from the main road. Parking their car, they got out, stretched their arms and took in the fresh country breeze, which had a hint of horse manure. Ready for their first horse-riding experience, the lads headed towards an elderly bloke who was tethering a saddled horse to a railing.

Midway across, Nathan's eye caught a glimpse of a dusty old car parked in a side shed and nudged Dave. 'Geez, mate, take a look at that!' said Nathan, wide eyed. The two lads went for a closer look and found it was a genuine manual Brock Commodore.

Nathan knew enough about cars to recognise that he had spotted something special. His dad had had a string of HSV Commodores before recently buying a 1968 Chevrolet Camaro, so he knew the VC Brock was as rare as duck's teeth.

Only 500 VC HDT Brocks were produced between 1980 and 1981, made available in a choice of just three colours: Palais White, Firethorn Red and Tuxedo Black. The cars were adorned with unique red, white and black side stripes to pay homage to Marlboro, the Holden Dealer Team's main sponsor at the time. Of these only 69 VC Brocks were made in Tuxedo Black, and of those 69 only about a third had the M21 four-speed manual gearbox. Each car built also featured an individual build number stamped into the Momo steering wheel.

Nathan and Dave don't remember seeing the build number stamped on the Momo steering wheel, but it can definitely be seen in one of the photos although it can't be made out. The best guess is that this Brock is build No. 60/500 judging by the SR-060 Victorian number plates.

As you can see, this tired Peter Brock–inspired survivor needs some attention, but it could easily be revived without restoration. Look closely and you'll see the faded decals and tail lights from years of being exposed to the morning sun. The exhaust system is hanging in there but is slowly deteriorating with rust. A colony of arachnids has made a home around the Brock, surrounding the wheel arches, tow bar and spoilers with their webs. The rafters above the bonnet seem to be a favourite roosting place for wild birds that show their appreciation by dropping phosphate deposits directly onto the bonnet, which are no doubt slowly eating away at the original Tuxedo Black duco.

Chatting with the caretaker while preparing for their maiden voyage aboard a horse, the boys learned that the Brock had been parked there many years ago and, at the time of writing, was still currently registered but unlikely to be for sale. ∎

BELOW This Brock Commodore's original Tuxedo Black paintwork is being eaten away by phosphate deposits from disrespectful birds. The first VC HDT models were available in three colours: black, white and red.

HIDDEN IN PLAIN SIGHT

The Falcon GT was the most economical way for the everyday Aussie to drive a car just like their racing heroes did, but as with some other race cars of the past, there are a few Falcon GTs that have been parked up and practically forgotten. Here is just one example: a genuine 1973 Polar White XA Ford Falcon GT sedan that is sitting idle and is covered in dust and cobwebs, waiting for another chance to get back on the road.

It has been said that often the best way to hide something is to leave it in plain sight, and this XA GT barn find is precisely that. If you knew the exact location of this dust-covered muscle car

you would be staggered by just how close it is to busy thoroughfares, major highways and even a capital city! Sitting under a lattice-clad carport and surrounded by bits and pieces including a wheelbarrow and lawnmower, the sun glistens on the chromed rear bumper bar.

'My father bought it new back in 1973. He loved his cars; he even had his own race team!' James Harrington, the current custodian of the XA GT, explained. 'I haven't driven it for a bloody long time. I parked it there, and that's where it's staying.'

Taking a closer look reveals the XA GT Falcon is missing some badges. The famous 'GT' moniker that adorns the boot lid is gone, as are the big 351GT

badges from the front guards. 'Someone jumped the fence one night and stole them. One day they were there and the next day they were gone: pricks,' James remarked in disgust. 'I've started getting the parts that are missing, so I can make it right again,' he said, pointing at the steering wheel, which has been replaced with a rubber-coated sports-style wheel. 'It isn't perfect, but it is what it is: a real 65,000 mile GT.'

The name Ian Harrington might ring a bell to fans of motor racing in the 1970s and 1980s. Ian ran a business called Roadways Pty Ltd, a road-surfacing and bitumen-laying company that operates in Tasmania. They have laid plenty of road on the apple isle, such as national highways and major infrastructure projects including some of the famous tourist roads such as the Tarkine Drive along the west coast of Tasmania. One of Ian's passions was motor racing, which saw him initially sponsoring a race team and eventually taking over as team principal. It was successful, too, with Allan Grice driving for the squad at one stage.

It was no surprise that Ian bought this XA GT Falcon new, as he liked the parallels that could be drawn to the cars raced on the track. This car was one of the last XA GT Falcon sedans to be built, being car 1,820th from the 1,868 produced according to Australian Classic Car History Services.

James has no immediate plans to get the car back on the road, although he does understand it is definitely a desirable muscle car. 'Eventually I'll get it going. I need to clear up the yard and find somewhere to put my mower,' James said, tongue in cheek. 'It will end up with my niece in due course. I'm not interested in selling it; I'd rather it stays in the family,' he stated. 'But for now it can sit there. It gives the spiders somewhere to live and keeps them out of the house!' ∎

BELOW James, son of a former Bathurst 1000 race team owner, says this 1973 Polar White XA Ford Falcon GT sedan will stay in the family. It's not for sale.

FREDDY THE INTERCEPTOR

'Freddy' was a rare breed of XA Falcon specially built by the Ford Motor Company to uphold the law. Falcon GTs were built to go fast and GT-HOs were built to go faster, but the Interceptor was built to catch them all. Equipped with the big 351ci 4V engine, Toploader gearbox and bulletproof nine-inch differential, this Freddy retired from active duty in 1973 with the force but continued with civilian duties until retirement in 1988. Covered in dust for 30 years, Freddy is quite possibly the last unrestored 1972 Ford XA Falcon 500 Interceptor known in captivity.

A few years ago Chris met George at a car show by sheer chance. Chris had spent a lifetime hunting the whereabouts of the former Victoria Police, Highway Patrol 1972 XA Falcon Interceptor he owned back in the 1970s, and was chatting to George about cars in general when he mentioned he knew of an original, unmarked 351cid V8 four-speed XA Interceptor in blue with a white roof.

'Is there any chance I could take a look at it?' Chris stuttered with excitement. 'Let me find out for you . . . Yeah, sure,' George said. 'I'm the guy who owns it.' Chris was awestruck that one of the important Q cars had survived in original, unrestored condition, as he'd been searching for more than a decade to establish this breed's existence. This was like striking gold!

It was déjà vu for Chris seeing George's car, especially when he opened the door to see the exact same saddle trim and gearshift standing proudly between the bucket seats as the car he'd owned 40 years ago. George bought the XA Interceptor on 30 March 1973 from New Oakleigh Motors in Victoria after it was decommissioned. 'I saw the

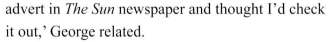

advert in *The Sun* newspaper and thought I'd check it out,' George related.

Freddy was built in May 1972, just before the Supercar scare, and sold new through B.S. Stillwell Ford in Kew. It was commissioned as a Victoria Police, Mobile Traffic Section Q unmarked Highway Patrol car on 27 June 1972 and disposed on 21 March 1973.

Apocryphally recorded on Ford Australia's files as a K code – 351/2-barrel-equipped Cleveland V8 – Freddy's ID tag is factory stamped as a T code, the same engine fitted to the Falcon GT, complete with the 4V Big Port heads. The L transmission code indicates the 28-spline Toploader four-on-the-floor, which drives to a slippery nine-inch complete with finned drums and XA GT–style tramp rods.

It's for this heavy-duty drivetrain that these Falcon Interceptors were aptly named 'Q cars' or 'Q ships', a wolf in sheep's clothing. Only two small 351 badges on each front fender hinted to something more special than a grocery getter.

The ID plate shows the colour code as G, denoting Blue Teal. In the box marked 'FR AXLE' the code U is unusually stamped, an anomaly that relates to the roof colour, which is Ultra White.

When George parked Freddy the car had travelled around 240,000 miles. When asked if he feared others finding out about where Freddy is stored, George replied, 'If anyone tries to steal it they better be able to run faster than a bullet, 'cause I'm a bloody good shot! In 240,000 miles I've changed the twin plate clutch, which was a bitch when reversing with a trailer, and the only mod I've made is adding the two cut-outs for the rear exhaust because the original exhaust tip drooped down like on a Fairlane.

> 'I was going to trade it in but back then they'd give me nothing for it.'

'Freddy's motor has never been pulled apart, although it's a little rattly on start up,' George said. 'I was going to trade it in but back then they'd give me nothing for it.' Luckily the XA was put away, as no doubt it would have been parted out for all its GT running gear. 'Other than a scrape on the rear quarter, the body is bloody straight. The paint is 100 per cent original,' George said.

George is in his seventies but is still actively working, and he has plans to revive Freddy one day soon . . . ▪

PART III:
going, going, gone . . .

RUST IN PEACE

Ever since Steve was a teenager travelling in his father's truck, he was always peering in different directions in an attempt to spot wrecks in the bush or an abandoned old car poking out from a farm shed. When he looks back now he realises this is how it all began and how he became a car hunter armed with his trusty camera always at hand. This is also how he stumbled across some incredible time-warp treasures.

'I'd been passing this vacant lot of old cars parked up in the bush around South Grafton, New South Wales since I was in my teens,' Steve said. 'Nothing gets me more excited than spotting an old car, and after all these years I finally decided to stop and ask permission for a closer look.'

When he did so Steve met Scott Jenkins, the owner of Heber & Hunter Auto Wreckers in South Grafton. Although his business is located in town this is Scott's own private collection, which he acquired over the decades with his late father Bill. Bill had a love of cars to a point where he had a tandem car trailer on a permanent hire basis.

Bill and Scott travelled the countryside looking for and rescuing old and not so old cars that were destined for the scrap metal yards. Sometimes they saved these sleeping beauties from farmers who were going to bulldoze them into dams! Scott said,

ABOVE Oh, my giddy aunt: how did this Torana hatchback end up here?
BELOW One can only imagine the stories behind the XA Falcon and the Monaro.

'Dad couldn't bear the thought of destroying such beauty.' Many of the cars pictured here are still complete; there are Buicks, Chevs, Fords, Holdens and Chryslers.

'It was like I was stepping back in time when Scott gave me the grand tour,' Steve explained. 'I could have spent hours upon hours just taking photographs and admiring the many different models. Each car has its own story of how and why it ended up here.'

Many of these cars have been sitting here for quite a long time and rust is consequently an issue, but there is still some gold in here worth saving. Scott understands he can't save them all and, as such, is pondering the thought of moving them on to someone who will restore them back to their former glory. ▥

SURVIVING CYCLONE TRACY

Christmas Eve, Darwin, Northern Territory, 1974: tropical Cyclone Tracy approached the city of Darwin with howling, gale-force winds. By Christmas Day she had unleashed her fury on the population, rendering 48,000 people homeless and leaving 65 dead.

Tracy made landfall at 3.30 am just north of Fannie Bay and barrelled through Darwin, demolishing everything in her path. At the height of her devastation all scientific measuring instruments failed when wind gusts surpassed 240 km/h. For a brief, 40-minute respite many residents had thought the worst was over, such was the false sense of security at the eye of the storm, but Tracy's fury returned with a fiercer vengeance, annihilating all that stood before her. Terrifying winds emitting a howling demonic roar as though jets were flying overhead.

For more than three hours, Darwin endured hurricane-force winds that tore off roofs, flattened dwellings, ripped trees from their roots, crushed cars and upturned planes. Flying debris sliced everything in its path. Hardly a home was left standing or unscathed, so savage was the cyclone's attack. Dwellings were beyond repair, communications were lost, power lines destroyed and water and sewerage were put out of action. More than 30,000

residents needed to be evacuated immediately by road and by air. This was the second time Darwin had been destroyed, the first being when Japanese air raids belted the city during World War II.

Among the survivors were the Bostocks, the uncle and aunt of Darwin resident Gavin Pocock. '"Big Red" was the name given to my late uncle Bing [Eric] Bostock's 1971 Falcon GT-HO Phase III, which survived Tropical Cyclone Tracy,' Gavin explained. 'Big Red was parked under the house at the time, next to my aunt's Toyota Celica, when the

AUSSIE CLASSIC CAR FINDS

cyclone hit. As you can see, the house was all but destroyed. Big Red suffered a broken back window and got bruised with a few dents and scratches. Building material debris was strewn everywhere!'

The elevated house was totally torn from its floor, leaving a safer haven for Big Red. After Cyclone Tracy, Uncle Bing had Big Red repaired and resprayed down in Katherine by a bloke who was the go-to panel guy back then. 'Uncle Bing was the second owner of Big Red and bought it around 1973. Big Red was well known around Darwin, and a force to be reckoned with both on the street and on the track. Uncle Bing drag raced Big Red at Livingston, the abandoned World War II airstrip, a lot during the 1970s.

'This was around the time the King Cobra Rod and Custom Club was born. The club has since changed its name and location and is now called the Hidden Valley Drag Racing Association, of which I'm vice president. Uncle Bing idolised Moffat's works GT-HO Phase III. Such was his passion that he even went to the trouble of adding a sticker kit to Big Red, replicating it as Moffat's No. 9 race car!

'We have a photo of the "Survivors" of Cyclone Tracy taken shortly afterwards. It shows Big Red in the middle, with my dad's silver GT on one side and a friend's [John Wilkie's] Vermilion Fire GT wearing 12 slots after it was stolen in New South Wales and recovered in the Northern Territory. In the background of this photo you can see the devastation caused by the cyclone. There are some other cool photos of Big Red in its heyday as well.'

Also pictured are other less fortunate cars unrelated to the story of Big Red that incurred Tracy's wrath. ▪

BOTTOM STRIP Big Red led a colourful life that included lugging boats and caravans plus being dressed up like Allan Moffat's race car.

RIVERLAND TREASURES

When you work as a livestock agent you get to see a lot of stuff no one else sees, and when you have hawk eyes for old cars you get to see some really cool and unusual car stuff.

Paddy Johns loves his job as a stock agent, especially when he gets to see old classic cars such as the ones he discovered across the Riverland in South Australia. The Riverland region spans almost 10,000 square kilometres along the Murray River and includes notable townships such as Renmark, Berri, Loxton, Waikerie, Barmera and Monash.

> *The farmers would often keep cars going for as long as they could, patching them up with repairs.*

With its Mediterranean climate and rich soil and the Murray as its water source, the area has been ideal for growing crops for many generations of farmers. In the good years many of these farmers rewarded themselves by buying cars, both for personal and farm use. A resourceful bunch, the farmers would often keep cars going for as long as they could, patching them up with repairs or buying other similar cars as spares.

Consequently, over time some of the farmers ended up with more than a few of each make and model.

Johns is a self-confessed car hunter who takes pleasure in photographing the cars he discovers. He and a work colleague with similar interests share stories and photos of their finds. 'I know of one farmer who has half a dozen coupes just wasting away in the grass,' Paddy said. His colleague likes to find classic cars and buy them. 'He recently found a '57 Chev that had been sitting for ages.'

This same colleague recently stumbled across a Lime Glaze with white trim XA Fairmont hardtop

parked in a paddock that most of us dream of finding. Sure, it's missing a few parts such as a door and grille, but it doesn't look too rusty and would be ideal for restoration if the farmer would ever let it go. And therein lays the problem: many farmers have amassed quite a few cars such as Holdens, Valiants and Falcons on their properties that they don't have a need or desire to sell, and many of these classics are just rotting away in the weather. 'On my trips out there I've found quite a few Chargers, but they're usually not for sale,' Paddy said.

If you ever find yourself travelling through the Riverland region, keep a sharp eye out behind houses and paddocks for old cars. There are plenty of them out there, and if you stop, knock and ask – you never know, you might just end up buying one. ■

ENTOMBED

ne night a few years ago down at the local hang-out known as Highway 31 Cafe, young Andy heard some talk about a bunch of old cars parked up a driveway in a nearby suburb and he decided he'd go for a look on his way home.

He was told to keep an eye out for a tired, yellow Holden VK Commodore sedan with broken tail lights that marked the spot where there were some gems parked in front of it. Driving slowly with high beams on, Andy spotted the landmark yellow Commodore. 'I chucked a U-bolt to check it out,' Andy said. 'It was pretty dark, and I could only make out a few cars, most notably an EJ sedan and a Torana.' Andy thought he'd leave the adventure for now and return in daylight hours for a closer look.

Andy went back the next day, and in the daylight saw four cars parked end to end as he walked towards the front door to ask the owner if he'd consider selling the EJ. 'I must've knocked for 10 minutes before the door was answered,' Andy related of the first time he met Frank, the owner of the gems. Andy told Frank he had noticed the old cars and asked if he might be interested in selling the EJ Holden. Frank cracked a smile before he answered, recounting the numerous times he'd been asked the same question before: 'They're not really for sale,' Frank replied.

Frank explained that he'd been driving the VJ Valiant ute when it eventually died, so he parked it up at the end of the driveway. Next he bought an LJ Torana with a factory four speed as a runaround until it too decided to give up the ghost years later. It was parked behind the Valiant ute, which had begun to have some serious rust issues with the floor collapsing in on itself. A small tree sapling had begun to grow between the Valiant ute and the Torana.

Frank went on to say he'd scored the EJ Holden, which he drove for a while until it also bit the dust. This was parked behind the dead Torana. Finally, Frank had bought himself a later model VK Commodore, thinking it might be a little more reliable, but after a few years it decided to stop running. Frank said it didn't worry him, as he was happy to catch public transport and no longer needed a car.

Andy was given permission for a closer look and a guided tour of the broken-down classics parked in the driveway. 'The EJ was pretty well rooted; she had a creeping vine growing inside it!' Andy said. 'The Torana wasn't much better, with rust holes everywhere and a plant growing up through the floor. She was basically a parts car. The Valiant ute was a rust bucket, beyond salvage. I think Frank was pleased to have some company, as I reckon by the looks of the place he didn't get too many visitors.'

Although each car had had its day Frank became quite enthused as he told the story behind each one, stating: 'One day I plan on getting them all going again . . .' Andy respected that Frank showed a true affection to each car. Frank finally added: 'When I get them going I'll then be able to get my father's old FB out of the shed.'

Andy looked around but couldn't work out what Frank meant, as there wasn't a shed to be seen anywhere on the property. 'Where's this FB parked?' Andy asked in curiosity, and Frank pointed to a large, overgrown bush not a metre from where they were standing. The overgrown bush had swallowed up the shed over the years and hidden it completely from view.

Frank explained that his father had parked the FB in the shed in 1976, and there it had stayed ever since. Andy asked how many miles were on the clock. 'Oh, about 40,000-odd,' Frank replied. 'I'll be buggered,' Andy gasped. Pushing aside some of the bushes and peering in, Andy could make out the old 1960 FB Holden Special sedan entombed in its final resting place. 'The shed had literally collapsed from the weight of the tree growth on top of and around the old girl,' Andy described of the scene before him.

Years went by during which Andy popped in from time to time to chat with Frank about the cars. Nothing had changed, and nothing seemed likely to change as Frank had lost interest as he was battling some serious health issues. One day Andy knocked on the door to speak with Frank. Frank's sister answered the door and gave Andy the bad news that Frank had passed away unexpectedly. Andy explained how he'd met Frank and that he had stopped by on occasion. Frank's sister said she'd be selling the estate and that she'd already done a deal with a local scrap metal merchant, who was collecting all of the cars in the next few days.

Driving past a few days later, Andy saw that the Commodore, EJ Holden and Torana were gone.

The rusted out Valiant ute remained but was now at the bottom of the driveway. The overgrown bush covering the shed had been cut back and the shed had been pulled down, exposing the FB Holden Special that had been parked inside since 1976, according to the last rego label. *What a damn shame*, Andy thought, as he would have loved to get his hands on this one. 'I just hope the scrap metal merchant had the brains to save it!' Andy said with some disappointment. ◼

ABOVE But wait, there's more . . . Quite apart from the line of Holdens out in the elements, there's an FB model trapped under the collapsed shed.

TOP SECRET SIX-PACKS

This book allows you to witness the last resting place of some very notable Chargers, two of which are Magenta-coloured R/T E38 optioned six-packs. These cars were parked up more than three decades ago, and until these photos were taken no outsiders had ever set on eyes them.

The location can't be disclosed, but it can be revealed that the Chargers lay in wait somewhere in rural South Australia parked outside and exposed to the elements save for well-weathered tarps held down by old wheels, a fuel tank and a bird cage. As can be imagined, after such a long period of time exposed to the harsh Aussie sun and driving rains their bodies have some corrosion, their paintwork is faded and the interiors are sun hardened and brittle but, regardless, their ID tags state they were factory built six-packs.

A whisper about these R/T E38s first reached the ears of some classic car enthusiasts awhile back, who rattled every chain they could to validate the rumour that the Chargers existed. They spoke to many a Chryslerphile, who were either tight-lipped about the R/T Chargers or truly didn't know they existed. After months and months of searching for a lead, the enthusiasts finally received a phone call from ever-reliable friend Michael, a self-confessed Mopar nut who provided a last name for the owner.

Everyone in the phone book with the same surname was called and gold finally struck, one old-timer hinting he was the person being sought. After grilling the enthusiasts with questions about who they were and what they wanted, the elderly gent finally felt comfortable enough to concede he had the Chargers. He indicated he would give access to the cars on the proviso the information about their location and owner was never revealed.

After half a day's solid driving the enthusiasts were met with an understandably lukewarm welcome.

They drove a further 30 kilometres out of town on a stinking hot day of almost 40 degrees on dirt roads; their host, who was nearing his seventies, must have been an ex-speedway racer as he took the bends at full speed in his trusty Falcon ute. They finally arrived at a typical country home with the traditional three feet high cyclone fence and barking dogs.

There were rusted out cars parked everywhere, from four-wheel drives to a Holden VR Commodore that had given up the ghost, to a tired old Merc that had one foot in the grave and the other on a banana peel. Among these beauties lay the object of the journey: four Valiants in a row, three of them Chargers, two of which were six-pack R/T E38s and the other a VJ 770 V8 coupe, and also a CM Valiant sedan with just 12,000 kilometres on the clock that looked like it had been hit by the Southern Aurora on one side when it was near new.

It's natural to wonder how these Mopar muscle cars ended up parked and forgotten for such a long period, but the long and short of it is that work and family commitments overtook the projects.

The first Magenta-coloured machine was an R/T Charger, No. 32 in production sequence, a rare J82 homologation six-pack. It was ordered through an unknown New South Wales dealer (Code N613) and sold new on 16 August 1971. It is one of 14 Magenta coloured R/T E38 six-packs built by Chrysler Australia Limited at their Tonsley Park plant in South Australia.

LEFT Sadly we can't tell you where these valuable Chargers are located, but we can tell you that the yellow machine was originally Magenta coloured.

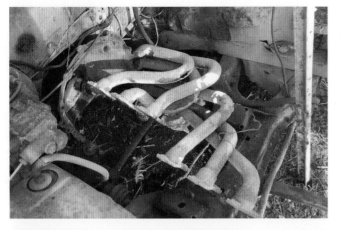

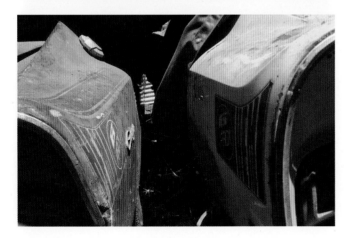

Being a desirable track pack it was fitted with twin fuel fillers, one on each side of the rear quarter panels. The dreaded tin worm had created havoc, with rust rotting through the sunburned paint on the bonnet. The grille was mangled and the boot lock had been pried open with a jimmy bar. The Charger was re-registered in South Australia in 1979 with SRV-968, but it had been out of registration for a long time. The tow bar indicates it was once used as a daily driver. The original engine (D363B0067) was now in storage in one of the many sheds on the property and was complete with the six-pack carb set-up. Sadly this E38 six-pack isn't a Survivor but is an ideal restoration project that is mostly complete. Being an E38, the gearbox is the trusty three-speed floor-shift manual.

No. 258 was one of 14 R/T E38 six-packs that left the factory painted Magenta with black vinyl trim, but along the way sometime in the 1970s someone changed it to bright yellow complete with painted bumper bars reminiscent of mid-1970s auto fashion. It was sold new on 14 September 1971 by Bob Walker Chrysler (Code N618) in Liverpool.

Missing the left-hand front guard and fitted with a blue bonnet from a donor car, the six-pack E38 engine (D363B00243) had also been removed and placed in safe storage. It also had surface rust all over from the moisture under the tarp, and the yellow paintwork was flaking off in large sections to reveal the pinky-purple hue of Magenta beneath.

The front bumper, grille and nose cone had damage consistent with hitting something such as a pole, and the damage to the right-hand rear quarter panel was indicative of how it met its demise. Although it was sold in New South Wales, this Charger was also re-registered in South Australia in 1978 with SDY-066. It had also been fitted with a tow bar, with the tow plug being drilled into the rear beaver panel.

This Charger was bought second-hand in 1977 in Ballarat for $1,500 without a gearbox. A three-speed gearbox was sourced at Barry James Wreckers and the car driven to

> *This Charger was bought second-hand in 1977 in Ballarat for $1,500 without a gearbox.*

Warrnambool. Two photos of this Charger when it was in its prime show it was painted yellow outside but the engine bay was still Magenta, with the six-pack E38 Hemi nestled in nicely.

The owner said he's too old to contemplate restoring the classics and is seriously considering a garage clearance sale, which will no doubt draw crowds from all over Australia. He also hinted he has another two E38s tucked away, one a Vitamin C and the other a rare Blond Olive six-pack, along with other Chryslers from the 1970s including a couple of E34 Pacers and Drifter panel vans. Imagine that. ■

BELOW It looks as though someone tried to break into the boot without a key.
BOTTOM The ID plate reveals that the pink Charger was one of just 14 Magenta-coloured E38s.

SOME DAY TOO FAR AWAY

magine a honey hole of classic cars that were squirrelled away one by one years ago before they were even considered classics. Most were driven in to storage but some were dragged in as they were no longer in running order. The long-term plan was and still is to get them all back on the road one at a time . . . some day.

Many readers will have come across a some-day barn find in their travels: an old but desirable car that has been parked up for a very long time, usually in a sad state of disrepair, that isn't for sale because the owner has plans to do it up some day and no matter what you say, you can't change the owner's mind about parting with it.

Sometimes the owner does have genuine plans to get the car back on the road but most times it's a pipe dream, and every day the car deteriorates more and its owner is not getting any younger. The intentions are good, but time has slipped them by.

Some owners like the thought of owning something somebody else wants. They like knowing that every week there'll be a knock on the door, or a note in the letterbox asking if they'd be interested in selling their car. Some day owners like to chat about their car and reiterate their plans to get it going again . . . some day. Sometimes, some-day owners are a little lonely and don't mind a chat about something dear to their hearts.

It's obvious that Mr Taylor loves old cars; after all, he's been accumulating them for ages. Sometimes they came to him from owners who knew he collected old cars, while at other times he'd gone out and found them for sale and bought them with an aim of doing them up some day.

Without realising it, one car turned into many. Call it an obsession, call it passion, call it what you like, but Mr Taylor couldn't resist buying an old car that one day he would do up. Perhaps it was cheaper to buy the dream of a classic car that needed work rather than purchase the reality of one that was already in mint condition, but at least this way it was more affordable to have many.

Not one to lean on a particular make or model, Mr Taylor loves all old cars equally and is fully aware of the values and desirability of some in his collection. He was happy for his collection to be viewed as long as its location was never revealed. On the day of the viewing the rain gods decided on a downpour. Many of the cars had been sitting for years at the mercy of such weather, becoming sunburned in the hot, arid summer and waterlogged when the rains came. Some had succumbed to rust and were now more suitable as parts or donor cars, while others were still unique or rare enough to be worthy of being restored or recommissioned.

LEFT That there's a rare Cortina GT.
ABOVE The Ford Fairmont XA GS Hardtop, optioned with the Grand Sport package, is at the top of Mr Taylor's list to restore.

All of the some-day barn finds came from different eras, starting from the 1950s and working their way up to plastic-bumpered newer models. Many were limited edition sports models that are nowadays hard to find. When Mr Taylor was asked what his plans were he answered: 'Oh, I slowly fettle away each day with one of them, and plan to get most of them on the road some day.' When asked if he'sdconsider selling them he said: 'Perhaps, if I got a good enough offer, but really I'd prefer to keep them as part of my retirement plan.'

Mr Taylor said he regularly gets asked to sell a car but has very rarely done so in the past. 'I buy more than I sell,' he stated. Some of the marques in this collection were truly awe-inspiring and many some enthusiasts would give up a kidney to own but, alas, these some-day barn finds are not really for sale.

Catching the eye was a Holden LC Torana GTR XU-1. Hot damn! It was a real GTR XU-1, albeit covered over with a tarp and protected by a vicious dog. This one was completed by Holden's Elizabeth Plant on 22 March 1971 and fitted with engine number 3100X-30252, although the engine and box have since been removed. Its dashing orange paintwork had since faded and was in desperate need of a birthday. Rust had eaten away the tail-light surrounds, and a new rear beaver panel is required. The inside of this one was quite untidy and needs complete reupholstering. To his credit, Mr Taylor has sprinkled Ratsak throughout to keep the mice population down.

There's also a Ford Mk1 Cortina GT. Red on red, this little GT has seen better days. It was missing its engine and gearbox but otherwise looks mostly complete, save for a few side stainless moulds missing. There was some of the other type of mould, the growth kind, that complements the rust as decoration.

As for the Ford Fairmont XA GS Hardtop, it's not for sale. This battered and bruised XA Fairmont hardtop has one foot in the grave. Optioned with the Grand Sport package, this Copper Bronze example has the faded remnants of the GS sidewinder stripe along its flank. The old tin worm has had a feast on the Ford's carcass, rust is evident in most of the lower panels and the panel behind the rear window has some huge holes. This one came from the factory with a 250cid six-banger, which looks mostly complete. Inside, it's a mess. The seats, dash pad and door trims look like they've been chewed up by dogs. Mr Taylor has this hardtop on his priority list of some-day cars to get back on the road and perhaps it could run again, but then again everyone wants a V8 in a hardtop these days. ■

TOP The Mini would certainly find a willing buyer if it was offered for sale.
ABOVE The hardtop Valiant is a rare machine indeed.

CENTURA

PART IV:
rescue missions

MOTHBALL EXHUMED

The story of Mothball is well known to car enthusiasts as the Holy Grail of Falcon GT barn finds, because this XA Falcon GT was parked up for more than 30 years and then eventually landlocked by a swimming pool, as outlined in an earlier chapter.

Mothball's owner Neil Wilkinson continued to thoroughly research his unique Red Pepper 1972 XA GT Falcon. Sadly, the latter stages of his investigations were done without his good friend and trusty sidekick Dave, who had passed away. Neil and Dave often talked about getting Mothball back on the road, but unfortunately time got the better of them and the car stayed exactly as and where it was.

Some car enthusiasts ultimately approached Neil to ask if he would consider putting Mothball into an upcoming car show, the inaugural Shannons Survivor Car & Barn Find Show Spectacular. After giving it some thought and discussing the concept with his family Neil agreed it was time to get Mothball out of the shed, more than 30 years after it had been parked.

This was easier said than done, as Mothball was between a pool and a hard place. The garage was not accessible by traditional methods, and with a large garden and swimming pool blocking the way, simply rolling the car out and pushing it down the driveway was not within the realm of possibility.

The idea of removing the pool fencing and placing steel beams and planks across the swimming pool was a possibility; however, after the length of time it had been parked the car may not roll effectively and might get stuck or, worse, fall into the pool!

The only feasibly safe and secure way for Mothball to be exhumed was to crane lift the car over the roof of the house and onto the street below, but with the

ABOVE LEFT Mothball's rescue via crane drew news crews.
ABOVE It would not have been a cheap exercise to extract Mothball from its landlocked shed.

street full of large and leafy trees plus power lines and telephone cabling, it was going to be extremely difficult. After consulting and discussing the situation with specialist crane company Rigweld, a plan was put in place and permits obtained from the local council. A date was set: Mothball finally had a chance to be retrieved.

On the day of the crane lift Neil invited his family and close friends to witness the event. They'd all known of the car for many years, and knew that it held a special place in Neil's heart. Racing legend Allan Moffat was also invited to witness this monumental event; given his connection to the Falcon GT nameplate, it seemed fitting. The media had also arrived to watch it all unfold, with the three major television news channels running stories on their nightly 6 pm news programs. This led to more than 2.5 million views on one story alone online: Mothball had gone viral!

As the crane arrived onsite and set up in the street, there was one major problem: Mothball was still inside the shed. It took a chainsaw, an angle grinder and a few strong men, but within minutes the fence between Neil's home and his next-door neighbour was removed, as was the wall of his double garage. This was the first time the front of the car had seen sunlight in over three decades. After spreading some crushed rock around and carefully laying some concrete pavers, Mothball was slowly pulled out of the garage, with Neil behind the wheel carefully steering his beloved car through the sharp metal and overgrown trees.

Cheers and applause followed as Mothball rolled from the garage into the grassy yard next door, to huge sighs of relief from all involved. Step one was complete, but step two involved way more risk.

A steel platform was lowered into

> **"**————————
> *This was the moment when the entire operation was held in the balance.*

the backyard by the crane, and Mothball was carefully loaded and strapped down onto it. This was the moment when the entire operation was held in the balance, and family and friends scrambled to get the best view as the crane slowly lifted the car into the air. After many months of planning, the lift began with the car on top of the platform being dangled high in the sky, across the roof of the Wilkinson family home and ever so slowly towards

ABOVE Ceremonial crane driver Allan Moffat was called in to add some celebrity factor to the proceedings. Mothball's extraction was timed to promote a car show.

the street below. Two drones appeared and followed the move, and thanks to the media interest there was plenty of incredible footage and photographs captured. This was a moment not to be missed.

By the time the car was ready to land on the street below, quite a crowd had gathered to see what all the fuss was about. It didn't take long before Mothball was back on the ground, after some skilful work from Ray the crane operator and his spotters and with a little help from 'celebrity crane operator' Moffat. Once the car was back on terra firma it was loaded onto a tilt tray supplied by Hop-Tow It and moved to a secure location to ensure the car

remained exactly as it was found, dust and all. After a few days in hiding, Mothball was then loaded into a fully enclosed transporter with PCD Transport and delivered to the show.

Mothball was now finally ready to be seen at the Shannons Survivor Car & Barn Find Show Spectacular, where it was showcased in all its glory and eventually crowned the best barn find in the show. ■

GRANDMA-SPEC TORANA

Edith Galloway finally upgraded her tired old grocery getter, a 1954 Vauxhall sedan, in 1971 for the Cinnamon Brown LC Torana S depicted here. The brown Holden served her well for some two decades, until it was parked up in the shed. And there it sat unused until recently.

Edith was a country girl who grew up near the Loddon River in the Mallee region of Victoria. She later became a farmer's wife before moving in 1952 to the industrial city of Geelong with her husband Alexander. In 1971 as semi-retirees they visited Smiths Holden, the local dealership located on Moorabool Street, Geelong, and traded in their beloved Vauxhall for a gleaming Torana S that sat proudly on the showroom floor.

The Torana was optioned up with a fan-boosted heater for those crisp bayside mornings. The only other additions were mud flaps, a driver's side weather shield and the mesh style sun visor, which offered some relief on hot days. Rather than opt for the four-cylinder version of the LC they chose the Torana S version, which came standard with the 161ci six-cylinder engine. The unassuming brown Torana had plenty of get up and go especially when compared to the old Vauxhall, which struggled to get up to the speed limit on a downhill run – with a tail wind!

The Torana S offered the best of two worlds, with big-car performance and small-car economy.

After Alexander passed away in 1989 Edith very rarely used the Torana, and only to pop up to the local shops for bread and milk. Eventually she had no use for it so she asked her son Don to park it in the shed, where it remained. This was around 1999, but Edith insisted it be kept registered in case she ever needed it one day. Besides, she didn't want to hand in the original registration plates.

When Edith also sadly passed away her Torana remained in the shed; the last registration sticker affixed to the windscreen showed 2008. The Torana was left to Don, who didn't have any specific plans for it.

Sitting for so long doesn't do an old car any good, and eventually the fluid in the brakes gave in. Over the years the Torana became something of a leaning post and storage shelf for all things kept in the shed. The tyres were old enough to vote by this stage and felt a little deflated all round.

> *The tyres were old enough to vote by this stage and felt a little deflated all round.*

Around 2016, Don's daughter and Edith's granddaughter Cindy and her husband Mark went to Don's on one of their regular visits and mentioned their interest in getting Nanna's car back on the road.

ABOVE Edith and Alexander Galloway were the first owners of this Torana. Incredibly, the car is still in the family.

'What are you going to do with Nan's car?' they asked. 'I'm happy for you two to have it as long as you don't change or modify it,' Don replied. This was good news but, as Mark and Cindy led quite busy lives, the Torana sat for another two years. Then Don passed away and the entire house block needed to be cleared.

With help from his good mate Ted and others, Mark got busy clearing all the stuff off the body of the Torana. With a trailer on hand, the dusty classic

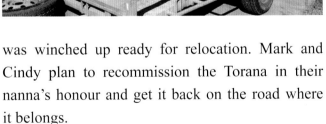

LEFT AND ABOVE After being used as a storage shelf for so long, Edith's brown Torana finally had the sun shine upon it. Her granddaughter has special plans for it.

was winched up ready for relocation. Mark and Cindy plan to recommission the Torana in their nanna's honour and get it back on the road where it belongs.

'We'd rather preserve the originality, especially as it has a genuine 60,000 miles on the clock, rather than restore it,' Mark, who well understands they're only original once, said.

'My dad loved the family farm,' Cindy explained, 'and when the Torana is back on the road we'll transport his ashes back to there, where he wished them to be spread.' ∎

FIND OF THE CENTURA

When Dan Barbary received a text message from his old man Brett, he had no idea it would lead him on a solo, 1,600 kilometre return journey to visit his late great-grandmother's farm in central Victoria to buy the original 1975 Chrysler KB Centura Sports Pack described here.

Dan, from Canberra, was out to dinner on a family holiday in Sydney when he opened a text from his father that simply read: 'Look what I found!' It was accompanied by a very dark, blurry photo of what Dan could just make out to be a Centura. 'It was quite possibly the most non-detailed picture of a car you could imagine,' Dan recalled, 'literally only the rear foot of the car was visible.'

Brett, who lives up near Dubbo and hadn't been to visit the old family farm in years, gave Dan a vague rundown of the dust-covered, mid-sized beauty but Dan, who is well versed in Centuras (he owns a highly modified nine-second KC Centura), still couldn't determine from the information at hand if it was a KB or KC.

Regardless, Dan was interested in buying the car that had been sitting in the shed on his great-grandmother's farm for some time so Brett called his cousin Jeff, and the search began to uncover who owned this mysterious Chrysler. A few weeks

went by before Dan finally discovered it was owned by his grandfather's brother Clem and prior to that by Clem's mother-in-law Vera Hatch. When Vera passed away in 2002 Clem had thrown five gallons of fuel in her old chariot and parked it up in the shed, where it sat unused until Dan's father spotted it 17 years later.

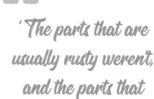

'The parts that are usually rusty weren't, and the parts that are always rusty had minimal rust.'

Dan called Clem to discuss the Centura's fate. 'I got told to have a number in mind and to be ready to do some kind of deal,' he recalled of their conversation.

The day to start the 800 kilometre long trek to the old farm finally arrived and Dan loaded up on supplies and had his trailer hitched onto the family's Grand Cherokee. After an overnight stay in Moama, he got to Clem's place bright and early and had a cup of tea, then they went out to the farm together. After a short while he found himself at the shed door, and the wait to see what he had gotten himself into was finally over. Upon lifting the door, he saw a car covered in dust and with a Masonite sheet on the bonnet that had fallen from the ceiling. He circled the car to take everything in before anything else.

ABOVE Adelaide-built Chrysler Centuras are as Aussie as a foot full of bindies, but they live in the shadow of their bigger Valiant siblings. This one lived in the same shed for almost two decades.

'I figured out pretty quick that it was a KB, and it was in very good, original condition,' Dan said. 'The parts that are usually rusty weren't, and the parts that are always rusty had minimal rust.'

Dan knew the mid-sized package from Chrysler was the higher-ecc'd GL model, distinguished by the rear bumper overriders, console, tachometer and low-fuel light and optioned with the vinyl roof, which was only available in GLs. Unfortunately, though, Dan could only inspect the interior through the windows. 'Know a good locksmith, do ya?' Clem cheekily asked as he explained to Dan that they could not locate the keys.

Despite this, Vera's Centura saved the best surprise for last, because when Dan popped the bonnet he discovered the little Chrysler sported the bigger Hemi four-litre donk! While the car appeared to be a sports pack, with the styled wheels and side stripe, Dan couldn't be sure as it was common for dealers to dolly up their models with similar styling. He called his wife and had her check the numbers while he was on the long journey back

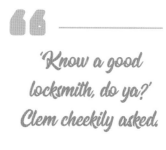

'Know a good locksmith, do ya?' Clem cheekily asked.

home. The numbers confirmed it definitely was an A55 Sports Pack, which included the additional wood-grain dash and Boca Raton cloth trim inserts.

After getting the car, which shows 98,184 kilometers, home and inspecting it some more, Dan was sure it was on its first trip around the odometer: 'The paint within the rear wheel wells is still bright, and overall it just doesn't look like it's travelled that far.'

Along with his highly modified KC Centura, Dan intends to keep this original beauty and has plans to get it re-registered and back on the road where it belongs, being used on the odd run to work and on weekends. ■

LEFT The six-cylinder Hemi-engined Centura packed a reasonable punch.
BELOW: How good does the black vinyl roof look on the lime body, especially after a wash?

LUNCH MONEY

'Frank!' a loving mother called to her 12-year-old son back in late 1971. 'Don't forget your money for lunch!' Frank Seychell rushed back to grab the money then rushed off to school.

'I never spent all of my lunch money,' Frank remembered. 'I had a dream. I had watched the GT-HO Phase III Falcons race around Bathurst. I was going to save and work my guts out to have what I wanted most: a GT-351. I loved cars. I got a panel beater-spray painter apprenticeship and was getting 16 dollars a week. It was bugger all. I saved and I saved. My mates bought cheaper EH and HR Holdens and told me to do the same. They called me a tight arse because I wouldn't spend a cent, but I knew what I really wanted.

'When my older brother Gatio bought his XW GS Falcon I was in awe. I wanted one more than ever,' Frank smiled. 'Then this newspaper ad appears around 1977 for an original 1971 XY Falcon GT for 5,000 dollars. I had saved 4,000 and it was an incredible amount for a 17-year-old to have. The guy in his 20s needed 4,600 dollars and I hoped I could negotiate.

'I headed over with Gatio and the GT was immaculate. The guy wouldn't budge, as part of his house had caught fire and he needed the money for the repairs. I was so close to my dream but I just didn't have the money. Then Gatio places his hand on my

ABOVE The garage was literally falling down around the valuable Falcon, so it had to be shifted. Watch out for those falling bricks!

shoulder and says, "I'll lend you the six hundred." I couldn't believe it was happening: I handed over the 4,600. I didn't even have my licence yet and I now owned this perfect car! Mum and Dad didn't know a lot about cars or they probably would have objected. Gatio had his XW and they just thought it was normal.

'I got my licence and was instantly popular with my mates. The first big drive we all did was to Geelong and we got lost. The fuel gauge was getting lower and lower and I told my friends that if they didn't put in for fuel no one was getting home. It was a great time to be young and own a GT-351. My mates and I would head down to Cherry

Lane and drag race. My dad would tap me on the shoulder then point at my rear tyres and say, "Son, what is wrong with your tyres? They are worn out." I'd just shrug my shoulders and say, "Cheap tyres, Dad. I'll get better ones next time." Dad would nod then keep walking.'

Like any young buck back then Frank drove the GT every day after he turned 18, adding some custom day two mods along the way such as front and rear HO spoilers, widened chromed slotters, tinted windows and go-fast performance bits on the engine. There's a tow hook mounted to the front of the car, and Frank attests to running the beast at Calder Park drags a few times. Then there were the times he couldn't help being a hoon on the street, ripping the odd burnout because those were the things you did back then.

'There was this girl I was keen on; her name was Karen. I thought I'd impress her by turning up at the drive-in in the GT. I took one look and thought, *"Bloody hell! I'm really punching above my weight."* The night was going well, and when we left I thought I'd impress her with my driving skills. I dropped the clutch, planted the accelerator and fishtailed all the way up the street. The only thing louder than the 351 was Karen's screams.

She'd never been in a car like the GT or with a teenage rev head behind the wheel. 'I thought I ruined any chances but I mustn't have, because we got married and I started building the family home.

Money was so tight, then we found out we were expecting our first child and I decided I didn't have a choice: I had to sell the GT. Karen put her foot down and wouldn't let me make a decision she knew I would regret for the rest of my life. Blokes kept offering *big* money but Karen wouldn't let me sell it.

'I couldn't afford to keep the GT registered or the insurance, so I parked it in Mum and Dad's garage in 1989. It was only going to be for a couple of years. Five years passed, then 10, then the years rolled on. I had two adult kids and a happy life with Karen. Dad and Mum both passed away but I couldn't bear to take the car away from their house: it was as if I was taking something away from them.'

Over the years Frank built up a matching-coloured Vermilion Fire GT-351 replica ute that he used as a daily driver until recently, when he pulled it off the road for a freshen up. 'The old garage was starting to crack and I knew I had to move the car. Michael,

my son-in-law who's a mechanic, and his mates organised a car trailer and shored up the front of the garage with supports. It was a delicate operation but we got the car back to Michael's house. Within a week the front of the garage collapsed,' Frank said. 'If it wasn't for the crumbling wall, the GT would have stayed where it was.

'I'd been busy working on my new business, FH Classic Auto Parts, something that came from helping Michael restore his VH SS Commodore. Karen had organised a barbeque at my daughter Emma and Michael's place, and we're all standing around looking at the GT. Karen says, "Why don't you sit in it?" So I sit in it and look at the key in the ignition. "Try starting it!" Karen said. So I just turned the key, and suddenly the engine rumbled into life. The sweet sound of 351 cubes filled the carport.

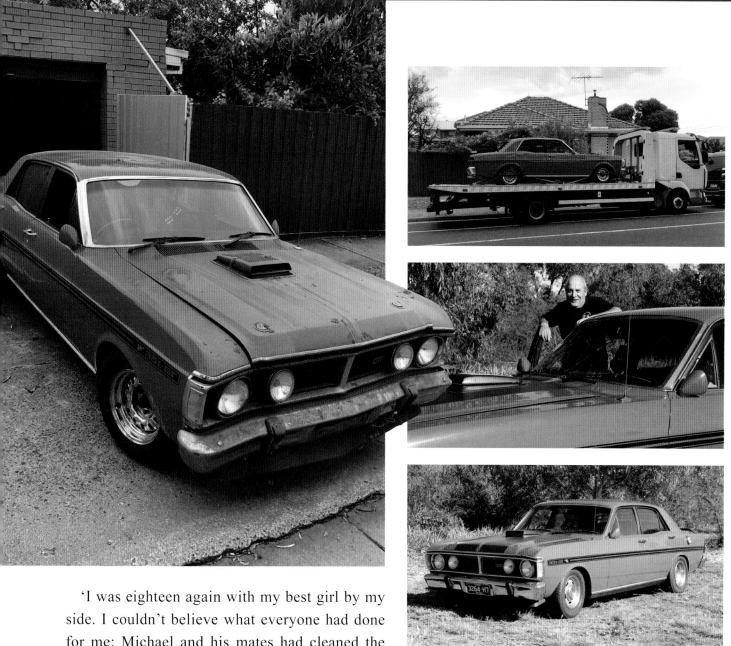

'I was eighteen again with my best girl by my side. I couldn't believe what everyone had done for me: Michael and his mates had cleaned the tank, recored the radiator and tuned the car. It's now got club rego and I think I'm taking a certain someone to the drive-in – and no fishtailing on the way home . . . maybe.' ∎

ABOVE The old girl ultimately scrubbed up well. We hate to think what might have happened if it had been left in the garage.

NEEDLE IN A HAYSTACK

A few years ago my friend Ange told this car enthusiast a bizarre story about an old car he found while on a hunting trip. His vehicle had broken down and he and his brother walked to the nearest farm for help. When the farmer took them into the old barn to get some tools, my friend noticed a dust-covered old car parked inside. Not being into cars, he didn't know what make, model or year it was.

Ange knew I was into old cars as he'd seen me driving one on many occasions. He described the car he'd seen in the farmer's shed: 'It was bluish silver and had flat tyres.' He wasn't sure of the make but thought it could have been a Holden. 'It looked like it had been there for years, it was covered in that much dust,' he said.

I asked if he remembered seeing a badge or anything on the car, to which he replied: 'It had a badge on the front like two flags or something. It had a stripe along the top across the bonnet and down the back.' This was now getting interesting, as anything with a stripe could be some sort of muscle car. Ange explained that he hadn't had much time to have a good look at the car as the farmer had grabbed the required tools ready to exit the dark shed, but he did add that he wiped the window with his hand to look inside and

remembered a blood-red interior and a clock on the console near the gear shifter.

I had begun to narrow down in my head what make and model the car might be, and asked Ange how many doors the car had. When he replied it was a two door I suspected it could well be a GTS Monaro coupe but

was stumped at what else it could be. Ange couldn't remember the address of the farmhouse and could only give me an approximate location of the nearest town, which was hours away on a dirt road. He did mention that the property had its own airstrip. Ange explained that his brother had arranged the trip through a shooter's club and the property they were camping at was listed in the club's booklet. I wanted to follow this up just in case the car in the barn was something special and not just somebody's custom-built hack.

I dropped in to Ange's brother's workplace a few days later and explained my interest in the old car that they'd spotted up near Tilpa. He vaguely recalled the car but hadn't taken much notice of it at the time as he was more focused on fixing Ange's broken-down vehicle. He found the booklet I was after under a pile of paperwork and said the place they had stayed at was one of six phone numbers listed on the inside back page. I called each of the numbers, the fourth one confirming it was the property the brothers had camped at. I asked if they knew of a nearby property with an airstrip, and the person on the phone confirmed there was one property about an hour away with an airstrip and gave me the property owner's number.

I spoke to a middle-aged fellow and explained my interest in the old car in the shed. 'Yeah, that was my granddad's car, he died in 1975,' he told me. I asked what make and model it was and he confirmed it was indeed a Monaro coupe. 'Call my mum, she lives in Canberra and knows more about it,' he said.

I called the number and spoke with Pat who, despite her age, was as sharp as a tack. She told me that her father had bought it new in 1969 from the Bowden Brothers Holden dealer in Bourke. 'I went with my father to buy that car,' Pat said. 'I was

ABOVE The 1969 GTS 327 is out of the farm shed for the first time in decades.
RIGHT The car still has its original NSW number plates.

40 years old then but remember the day like it was yesterday.' She confirmed that her father had bought a silver-coloured Monaro with the 327cid V8 motor after a good year's farming. 'My father was old fashioned and never liked radial tyres. He made the dealer swap the wheels from a standard Kingswood.' I later learned she meant this Bathurst GTS 327 Monaro was delivered with standard cross-ply tyres and standard hubcaps.

When I asked if she might be interested in selling the Monaro she said she would have to speak with her other two sisters, as they had been left the car as an inheritance when their father passed away in 1975. The Monaro hadn't been moved in decades, but Pat assured me it had been started occasionally.

A few days later Pat called and nominated a non-negotiable price that had to be paid by bank cheque, making it clear she wouldn't accept a cash payment. I asked her just how good the Monaro was, to which she replied it had some 45,000 original miles on the clock and was like new save for a dent in the front guard where her dad had hit a roo and some gravel rash along the lower side panels from being on dirt roads all its life. I mulled it over and eventually agreed to pay Pat the asking price without seeing the car on the proviso the car was left untouched and unwashed until I got there. She said she'd arrange for her husband to fly his Cessna from Canberra and meet me at the sheep station, which her son now managed. The sheep station was quite impressive, consisting of the homestead

built in the early 1900s encompassing 55,000 hectares with some 14,000 sheep.

I arranged for my good friend and experienced truckie Brian Russell to hook up his trailer and join me on the 2,000 kilometre round trip adventure. As car hunters, we were about to make history in finding the Monaro in the barn. After many hours of driving we turned down a 2 kilometre long driveway with the airstrip to our left and a Cessna aircraft parked at the end of the runway. I caught

> 'When I opened the driver's door I was knocked out by the sight of the Goya red interior.'

sight of the Monaro, and my heart started to beat dents in my chest. I was excited.

We were greeted by Pat's husband, who apologised for the Monaro being so dirty. When I opened the driver's door I was knocked out by the sight of the Goya red interior: although it was a little dusty it was still like new. I handed the bank cheque over to Pat's husband.

I had just bought a Silver Mink Holden Bathurst GTS 327 Monaro, which turned out to be one of

Aussie Classic Car Finds

six known with a factory-fitted vinyl roof. Being a 1969 model, it was the Series 2 version with the higher horsepower engine. The Monaro had 45,228 miles on the clock, and to this day is believed to be the lowest-mile unrestored HK Bathurst Monaro in existence. Unfortunately, Pat's husband had pumped up the tyres as a courtesy while it was still in the shed and it bothered me that the front guards and bonnet were a slightly different shade to the rest of the car, but I later learned about dirty flip sides in the paintwork, which explained everything and put my mind at ease.

> The Monaro had 45,228 miles on the clock, and to this day is believed to be the lowest-mile unrestored HK Bathurst Monaro in existence.

Pat's husband started the Monaro and it burbled to life with a nice V8 rumble and a slight exhaust leak. It was hard to believe this car had been parked in the earthen-floored shed since 1975 hundreds of miles away from civilisation. Pat's husband hosed off the Monaro and Brian and I loaded the old girl onto the tandem trailer for the long trek home.

LEFT If anything the layer of dust served to protect the car's paintwork.
BELOW The HiLux ute hit a kangaroo on the trip out to fetch the Monaro.

The trip home went smoothly, but at every fuel stop we were approached by rubberneckers for a closer look. Most were shocked to hear the Monaro had been sitting in a shed for so many years and there were quite a few offers to buy it right there and then that were politely declined.

Once it was home the Monaro's brakes were recommissioned and it was given a good tune-up and service. It was then entrusted to my good friend Laurie for detailing, with him explaining the dirty flip side in the paintwork where the front clip of the car was painted separately from the rest of the Monaro at the factory and then fitted later during production. Because the metallic paintwork was applied on a different angle to that of the rest of the car, after years of oxidisation the paintwork appeared mismatched. This was rectified after a thorough cut and polish. I elected to keep the Monaro coupe as original as possible, so the small dent left from the kangaroo Pat's dad had hit on the passenger guard was left untouched, as was the gravel rash along the sill panels. A set of GTS wheel caps and red sidewalled tyres were added to the Monaro. It still smelled like a new car inside!

Word soon got out about this incredibly low-mileage Monaro Survivor, no less than a 1969 Holden HK Monaro GTS 327, and it wasn't long before collectors and enthusiasts started calling to check it out as a reference car and to make offers. After receiving a very handsome offer that had the impact of changing my life and that of my family, I made up my mind to accept it as I felt guilty with each mile I had put on the Monaro so far. It was time for the old girl to go to someone whose lifestyle was better suited to having a car as a museum piece. Besides, I had just heard about another muscle car that had been sitting in a shed for decades, covered in dust and with flat tyres, but that's another story for another time . . . ■

LEFT We had hardly noticed the black vinyl roof until the car had a proper bath.
ABOVE That's a pristine interior!

BIRDS OF A FEATHER

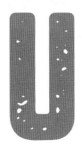sually rivals like Holden and Ford would be fighting like cats and dogs, but here were two beauties silently sleeping together. As the eyes of these car enthusiasts adjusted to the dim light, we began focusing on the finer details the 1975 Holden HJ Premier and the 1978 Ford XC Fairmont GXL.

A sight to behold, both cars were fully optioned and both had the big V8 motors: the HJ was the 5.0 litre and the red Ford the 5.8 litre. Both were top of the line models: Premier and Fairmont GXL. Both were hamburgers with the lot, and both had factory sunroofs . . . Let's rephrase that:

both were hamburgers with the lot, with pineapple on top!

Back in its heyday the Prem was the duck's guts. Whoever ordered it must've been flush with cash and wanted to make a statement, as every option box was ticked: Absinth Yellow paint – check; big L31 V8 – check; turbo 400 auto – check; air, steer, power windows and aerial – check; GTS steering wheel and instrumentation – check; sunshine roof (Option C03) – check!

It had last been registered up until 1 October 2000 and has sat unused for some 17 years. Mice and rat poo was strewn all over the engine, no doubt the rodents having made lunch out of the wiring.

The water bottle was now a penthouse mouse nest. The interior was in surprisingly good condition except for a few paint stains on the carpet, and the seats were protected with seat covers. More than 269,000 kilometres were showing on the clock, but the original black and white Victorian number plates IHD-598 had never left the car. Cragar mags, wearing dead flat but quality performance tyres for the era, are slowly being swallowed up by the earthen floor.

This car held sentimental value for the family and will not be sold. This, however, was not the case with the GXL.

The Fairmont GXL is fast becoming a rare and highly desirable classic. It's just not seen on the road as much as it used to be, most having been parted out for their heavy-duty running gear or rusted away. Finding one in a hero colour such as this Flame Red barn find is even rarer. Once again, whoever wrote the cheque to buy this one when new knew exactly what they wanted and weren't short of a dollar. As the top of the line luxury model in the sedan range, this XC Fairmont GXL was loaded with options. First was the massive 5.8 litre V8, FMX automatic (since changed to a floor shift four-speed manual) and the big Ford nine-inch diff with four-wheel disc brakes. Add to this power steering, air-conditioning and wind-back sunroof, which makes it one flaming, red-hot package.

The comfort of corduroy chamois-coloured trim had been enjoyed by some large-sized rats by the looks of the souvenirs they'd left behind. A sports steering wheel and aftermarket Speco shifter was fitted and the windows were wind-ups. Surprisingly, there are only 89,563 kilometres showing on the odometer, all of which are claimed

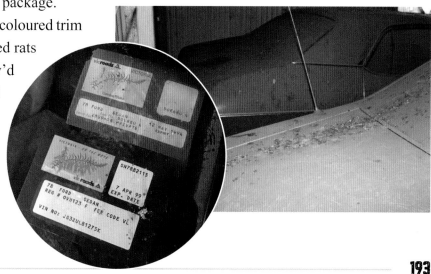

to be genuine. Given the condition of the body, and although the car is covered in dust and stained with heavy bird shit on the boot lid, it's more than likely the mileage is genuine. Built in January 1978, the GXL had sat unused since 7 April 1999: talk about a long slumber! Chrome 12 slots common as a day two mod in the 1980s were fitted. Some Ford enthusiasts call chrome 12 slotters 'Option 102' these days.

These cars once belonged to Thomas James Howe, or 'TJ' as he was known. Born in 1968, TJ was only 47 years old when he passed away. Quite the eccentric, he dressed in his long leather jacket and big cowboy hat and had large chunky rings on every finger. Wherever he went people stared; kids thought he was a pirate similar to Captain Jack Sparrow. Even his doctor called him Pirate Tom. He loved the attention, and it wasn't uncommon for

TJ to hook up his horse Tuff to a 100-year-old buggy and head off 20 kilometres down the highway to the pub. His friends thought he was a lunatic!

TJ's son Jamie said: 'My school mates would say they saw my dad in his horse and cart,' to which he'd reply, 'No, that wasn't my dad!' He laughs about this now.

TJ bought the GXL from his father some 25 years ago. It had lived in the Mildura region most of its life, remaining relatively rust free. The yellow Premier belongs to TJ's widow Samantha: 'I liked yellow, and wanted a yellow car.' She drove it as a daily driver, taking a young Jamie to school. 'One day I let TJ drive it, and had tins of paint in the back on the floor. He said he was only going to the shop . . .' She continued: 'Full of it, I caught him doing burnouts down the road. He spilt all the paint on the floor and I had to use my new Vax to clean it, then

he wrecked the Vax too! I no longer allowed him to drive my car.' A year later the HJ Prem was parked up when Samantha bought a new car.

With no need to keep the Fairmont GXL, the family made the decision to move it on. Someone who was known to them had shown interest in buying it, making them an offer for the XT panel van (also in the shed) and the GXL as a package. The sale went ahead with the buyer agreeing to purchase them as a lucky dip, unsure whether they'd even start up or what they needed in the way of maintenance. He was transparent with his intentions, stating he would clean them up, get them running and move them on. After tipping in some resources to getting them both going, each was detailed and advertised for sale. They were snapped up instantly, especially given the rarity of the GXL. So what of the Premier? Samantha said: 'One day I'll do her up.' ▪

ABOVE Locked and loaded, the GXL has been sold.
BELOW Here she is all cleaned up, a real stunner.

MEET TWEETY BIRD

Sometimes barn finds aren't about muscle cars or super-rare classics but are about humble family sedans once owned by little old ladies. Such is the case with this 1974 Mazda Capella 1600 called 'Tweety Bird'.

In 1974 Gough Whitlam was Australia's prime minister, a new music show called *Countdown* hit our screens, *The Box* and *Class of '74* were the new TV soapies and Peter Weir's film *The Cars that Ate Paris* hit the big screen. As for the car industry, Mazda and other Japanese car makers were making some headway in Australia. Mazda offered small, economical, reliable vehicles generally carrying more gear as standard that were options in cars made by the big three. For families looking to buy a second vehicle, generally used as 'Mum's taxi', the small Japanese cars made sense.

For Edith there were more pressing issues to deal with. Her Holden Special sedan was proving to be unreliable and she was getting fed up with it. One day her Holden broke down in the main street of Warracknabeal, and that was the last straw. She made a beeline for the local Mazda dealership, Amor Motors.

Edith soon drove away in a brand new Mazda Capella 1600. Robert French, Edith's grandson, said that initially things weren't going that well for Edith and the Mazda: 'In the first few days of ownership she wasn't that impressed with the Mazda. She decided she would give the Mazda to her eldest daughter Ester, who was driving a Toyota Corolla and was going to use the Corolla as a trade-in for another car.'

According to Robert, after two weeks of driving the Mazda Edith changed her mind and decided she did like her Mazda after all. It was used for daily driving duties around the Wimmera and Mallee regions but did make some longer trips to Melbourne. Edith allowed Ester to also use the Mazda for light driving duties.

Edith drove the car until about 1999, by which time she was too old to drive safely; the Mazda was stored in a shed on a friend's farm. When Edith passed away the Mazda continued to sit in the shed because Robert and his family could not contemplate selling the car for fear it would be trashed by some young bloke looking to drop a rotary engine in it.

John Robinson was working as the heritage collection technician at Mazda Australia when he

BELOW Not all finds are muscle cars or super-rare classics.
RIGHT This Mazda sat all alone in a farm shed for 17 years.

AUSSIE CLASSIC CAR FINDS

was told by Wade Morrow, the principal of Morrow Mazda, about a Mazda Capella 1600 that had been sitting in a shed untouched for 17 years. Wade was a long-time friend of Robert French's. John contacted Robert and explained his role and that of Mazda Australia in collecting and preserving Australian-delivered Mazdas. Robert agreed to part with the car, comfortable in the knowledge that Edith would be more than pleased to know the car was on display with a collection of other Mazdas.

John and Wade pumped up the tyres on the Mazda, loaded it onto a trailer and took it to the Morrow Mazda dealership in Horsham. They washed off the dust and spiderwebs, changed the mud-clogged

ABOVE Tweety loaded up and ready to head to its new home – to Mazda Australia to be put on display.

fuel filter, put some fuel in the tank and hooked up a new battery. The car started and ran without missing a beat. The underside shots of the Mazda on the hoist show a well-preserved example. The paint had survived better than expected due to the layer of dust and being inside a shed for the last 17-plus years. All John and Wade did was pressure wash and chamois dry it.

The Mazda is quite a time capsule and a credit to Edith's careful ownership. The last registration label is dated 1999, the year Edith stopped driving. Overall the interior is in great condition, with the carpets showing some wear. Interestingly, the car has the standard original windscreen with inbuilt radio antenna but for some reason the optional AM radio was not upsold in the deal. Edith's Mazda Capella is a perfect addition to the Mazda vault, which prides itself on finding, maintaining and displaying Mazdas in original Survivor condition. ■

RIGHT Tweety's registration ran out last millennium.
BELOW This Mazda Capella is now part of Mazda Australia's Heritage Collection. The focus of the collection is not to create concours-standard cars but to retain an appearance in keeping with the age and former use of the car. What a little ripper!

VICTORIA · ON THE MOVE
vic roads
7
END DATE
12 JLY 1999

1974 MAZDA SEDAN
REG NO LWN110 X FEE CODE VL
TARE 900
ENG NO 61975
SN 1996854

Mazda Capella
MAZDA HERITAGE COLLECTION

Mazda Capella
MAZDA HERITAGE COLLECTION

EUREKA: GT GOLD!

With only 596 Falcon XR GTs built, finding one that had been sitting unused for 18 years covered in dust and cobwebs would be like striking gold – and, like any barn find story, without photos as proof it would be just another pub story. A good car hunter will always take photos of a find so there's never any dispute about whether the story is true or not.

Ross Vasse has been a car hunter for most of his life. He lives, eats and breathes cars – old cars. Not a day goes by when Ross isn't driving on an alternative route to most, looking up driveways and following up on every lead. It was one of these leads, a nugget of information from his good friend Walshie, that led Ross to finding this GT gold-coloured Falcon GT parked in a farm shed in Wedderburn.

To get to the farm Ross turned up the long, bumpy drive that looped around the back of a tired, weather-beaten timber home that had stood for almost a century, passing a few dead Kingswoods and a ute along the way. He was greeted by Neville, a bloke who was as old as the house and dressed in a faded navy singlet and worn blue jeans held up with a bit of rope. Ross said he had heard Neville had a few old cars lying around that he may be interested in selling. Old Nev started to rattle off a description of some of the cars on the property, mostly rust buckets with one foot in the grave and the other on a banana peel, then he mentioned a Falcon GT, a Corvette Stingray and a Monaro.

Keen to see these cars, Ross asked if there was any chance he could take a look, and Old Nev turned towards the shed. It was a huge hay shed open on one side and with a high roof two storeys up. The dirt floor was caked in a layer of dust that had been blown in by the wind and had little pockets where wild rabbits had dug around. Also covered in dust were all the cars, but the one that caught Ross's eye was the gold XR GT pushed up in a corner. Ross popped the bonnet and saw the engine was covered in dust and surface rust, but noticed the ID tag on the support panel and the JG33 numbers stamped into the radiator support panel. The number on the left-hand shocker tower matched the engine. Eureka: a matching numbers example!

Every car on the property was for sale except for the Falcon GT – of course. Ross was patient and kept in touch with Nev over the years; Nev always said that when he was ready to sell he would call Ross first. Late one night Ross got a phone call from Nev, who said: 'Hey, mate, if ya want that bloody XR be up here in the morning with some cash and she's yours.'

Ross arranged to borrow a mate's Chev truck and car trailer and was on the road at sparrow fart for the long trek out to the farm. Old Nev came out dressed exactly the same as he had been the first

'Hey, mate, if ya want that bloody XR be up here in the morning with some cash and she's yours.'

time and was probably a little under the weather from a tough night on the piss. Nev had already told Ross what he wanted for the GT, which was fair considering it hadn't run in years due to a leaking radiator.

Ross handed old Nev a bundle of Johnny Cash, who scribbled a receipt. It was time to get the XR GT out of the shed . . . or was it?

The old GT had sat in the same spot for so long the rear brakes were seized on completely but this didn't bother Nev, who hooked up his old XF ute to a rope tied under the XR's axle. The ute was screaming at peak RPM, with its tyres howling and digging themselves into ruts. Although the brakes on the XR didn't free up, the ute managed to drag it out into the light of day kicking and screaming. At one point Ross thought Nev wasn't going to stop but would keep driving down the end of the driveway!

The next problem was getting the Falcon onto the trailer with seized brakes, a problem that was solved by removing the drums. Locked and loaded and with a big wave goodbye, Ross headed for home. Plenty of rubberneckers slowed down for a closer look at the dusty and dirty XR GT tied down like a dinosaur on the trailer.

At one fuel stop a couple of punters even made offers to buy it on the spot, but Ross had other

> *The next problem was getting the Falcon onto the trailer with seized brakes.*

plans for the old girl: he planned to revive her.

About a week later Ross found himself a bit short of money but couldn't figure out why, then the penny dropped and he called Nev to ask if the cash he'd handed over had been the correct weight. Luckily Nev hadn't spent any of the money and came back on the phone, stating: 'I've just counted it and there's five grand more here than there should be.' Old Nev, who was as honest as the day is long, has sadly now passed on to greener pastures. ▥

BOTTOM LEFT Popping the bonnet revealed a matching numbers Falcon XR GT that had been parked for 18 years due to a leaky radiator.